MEDITATIONS FOR MEDIOCRE MYSTICS

*Inspiration for the Spiritually
Homeless and Hungry*

"We grow toward the person we wish to become and Tom Stella gifts us with a journey – a certain vision, a collage or a montage of intellect or reason, and that of simply seeing, thus appealing to both heart and mind on every page. We grow through his book part by part, page upon page because his idiosyncratic selections of quotes and commentary lead us to a denouement and theophany, serving those of us on a spiritual journey. Meditations for Mediocre Mystics most certainly is another brilliant piece of work from Tom Stella."

– Joseph Price, licenced psychotherapist,
teacher, spiritual follower, and writer

TOM STELLA

MEDITATIONS FOR MEDIOCRE MYSTICS

*Inspiration for the Spiritually
Homeless and Hungry*

WOOD LAKE

Editor: Mike Schwartzentruber
Proofreader: Dianne Greenslade
Designer: Robert MacDonald

Cover photograph: Luke Wass

A Cataloguing in Publication record for this book
is availabe from Library and Archives Canada

ISBN 978-1-77343-521-3

Published by Wood Lake Publishing Inc.
485 Beaver Lake Road, Kelowna, BC, Canada, v4v 1s5
www.woodlake.com | 250.766.2778

Wood Lake Publishing acknowledges the financial support of the Government of Canada.
Wood Lake Publishing acknowledges the financial support of the Province of British Columbia
through the Book Publishing Tax Credit.

Wood Lake Publishing acknowledges that we operate in the unceded territory
of the Syilx/Okanagan People, and we work to support reconciliation and challenge the
legacies of colonialism. The Syilx/Okanagan territory is a diverse and beautiful
landscape of deserts and lakes, alpine forests and endangered grasslands.
We honour the ancestral stewardship of the Syilx/Okanagan People.

Printed in Canada
Printing 10 9 8 7 6 5 4 3 2 1

CONTENTS

INTRODUCTION

All my life my heart has yearned for
a thing I cannot name.
— André Breton[1]

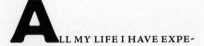LL MY LIFE I HAVE EXPE-
RIENCED THE YEARNING TO WHICH FRENCH WRITER
AND POET ANDRE BRÉTON REFERS. For me that yearning
is composed in part of a subtle discontent, a quiet feeling
that something is missing despite the fact that nothing is
missing. Significant relationships, meaningful work, material and monetary security have never been enough to satisfy the desire for that which I cannot name.

I know I'm not alone in my discontent or my longing
for the nameless, for mystics of every spiritual and religious
tradition have spoken of their desire for and experience of
union with a spiritual entity that is as real as it is surreal. I
am not claiming that because I share their yearning I consider myself a mystic, but neither do I believe that the term
"mystic" is entirely inappropriate for those of us who might
glimpse briefly what "certified" or canonized mystics have
been blinded by.

The term "mediocre mystics" seems a fitting way to refer to those who yearn for the nameless but do not qualify
as full-blown mystics. I realize that because there is nothing
middling about mystics, "mediocre mystics" may appear to

be an oxymoron, but the root meaning of "mediocre" is not second-rate. From the Latin *mediocris*, the word means *moderate* or *ordinary*, and has been used figuratively to refer to one who is halfway up a mountain. Unlike ordinary folks, sainted mystics have reached the mountaintop; they are on a first-name basis with the nameless! But just because we haven't arrived at the heights and just because our lives unfold in the valley of ordinary, everyday life doesn't mean that we do not experience the desire that has fuelled the mystic's climb. We may not realize it, but all mystics, whether ordinary or advanced, share a common yearning for the same nameless mystery.

I have found that my inability to name that for which I yearn can at times be discouraging, for it has made me doubt myself and wonder whether my being discontent with what satisfies most people is really just a matter of my being a malcontent. If this is your experience, too, I hope you are learning along with me to give yourself the benefit of the doubt. I have come to look upon my dubious thoughts and feelings as dark gifts, as opportunities to trust my heart's desire and to strengthen my resolve to continue the pursuit of "a thing I cannot name."

My experience, both personally and professionally, has led me to believe that many mediocre mystics are spiritually homeless and hungry. Because they no longer find meaning or inspiration in the rules and rituals of institutional religion, mystics (mediocre and otherwise) often leave their faith family as they search for a community of like-minded companions with whom to feast on matters of the soul. And although their longing for soul food and friendships may be unfulfilled, most continue the quest for the nameless. A heart's yearning is not to be denied.

A word about structure: I have divided this work into

five parts, each of which begins with an introduction and is made up of a number of meditations that consist of a quote followed by a brief commentary. Because spiritual matters are boundless, many of these meditations could have been appropriately listed under several of the following headings.

ONE: STEPPING TO THE BEAT OF A DIFFERENT DRUMMER

So much of what makes sense to mediocre mystics is out of step with the ways of the world; what makes soul-sense seems like nonsense to most people. The meditations in this section are countercultural; they are contradictory (against the word), for they affirm the rightness of thinking and acting "outside the box."

TWO: RESISTING THE PULL OF PERFECTIONISM

It is often the case that in our desire to become our best self we try too hard to attain an unattainable ideal. As with the other aspects of our being (physical, mental, emotional), in the spiritual life it's important to be clear about the kind of person we hope to become. As these meditations claim, however, it is essential to know that our imperfect self is good enough.

THREE: BEING AWAKE TO THE MYSTERY IN OUR MIDST

Because God can be understood as the spiritual essence of all creation ("ground of being"), our full presence to each moment positions us to be smitten by a sense of the holy even in the most mundane aspects of life. These meditations encourage being fully present to everyday life.

FOUR: A LIFE-GIVING PERSPECTIVE ON RELIGION

For millennia, religious institutions and teachings have been a beacon in the darkness for many. But also true is that formal religion has lost credibility in the minds and hearts of a growing number. When its teachings are viewed through a spiritual lens, religious renewal becomes possible. These meditations offer a different perspective on matters religious.

FIVE: DISCOVERING HOLINESS WITHIN

Because many of us tend to live busy lives, we fail to sense the spiritual depth that is most often encountered in quiet stillness. Also problematic is that words like "spiritual" and "holy" are often thought to refer to realities that are *beyond* rather than *within* us. Because that for which our hearts yearn is in part a connection with our soul, the meditations under this heading reinforce the truth that we are essentially a Sacred Self.

* * *

The recognition that my soul needs nourishment and companionship so as not to tire in its search for the nameless has led me to write and to offer these meditations as food for my journey and for yours. It is my hope that they will help to satisfy our spiritual hunger and that by sharing them with others they might become a catalyst for connection, conversation, and community – a hearth of words for a new spiritual home.

NAMING THE NAMELESS

It is my educated guess that many if not most of you have a name for the nameless – "God." I share the inclination to use this moniker, for I was taught that God is the name of a Supreme Being, someone who is a bigger, better version of ourselves.

But along with the inclination to name the nameless, I have a deeper instinct telling me that even a revered term like "God" falls short of the ultimate reality for which we yearn. Any name for the nameless limits Mystery, to which the word "God" refers.

For this reason, my use of "God" in the meditations that follow is not meant to denote a divine being who resides in the heavens, but to connote the personal, infinite, intimate spiritual essence at the heart of all creation.

ONE

STEPPING TO THE BEAT OF A DIFFERENT DRUMMER

EVERY CULTURE HAS ITS
CONVENTIONAL WISDOM, ITS UNQUESTIONED NORMS,
AND UNIVERSALLY ACCEPTED VALUES. In the Western
world, concepts like "more is better," "busy is good," and "success equals wealth," are examples. But just how wise it is to
embrace these standards is debatable, for it is often the case
that pursuit of a culture's values leaves one feeling more
empty than full, more depleted than completed.

In contradiction to conventional wisdom, are the teachings of priests and prophets, philosophers and poets in every
spiritual and religious tradition. Their understanding of a
full life is not about accumulating more but about doing
with less. It is not about being constantly on the go but about
living at an unhurried pace. And it is not a matter of fame
or fortune but of being self-fulfilled.

The following reflections articulate an unconventional
wisdom, a countercultural approach to life that makes soul-sense even as it may appear to be nonsense to the world.

A HIGHER LAW

*In Germany, under the law, everything is prohibited, except
that which is permitted. In France, under the law, everything is
permitted, except that which is prohibited. In the Soviet Union,
everything is prohibited, including that which is permitted. And
in Italy, everything is permitted, especially that which is
prohibited.*

– Newton Minow[2]

It may be because I'm Italian that I'm drawn to the above quote attributed to Newton Minow, an attorney and former chairman of the Federal Communication Commission. Unlike his assessment of the legal systems of other countries, Italy's approach to the law is one that posits a healthy regard for disregard. If its parameters are too confining, we may have not only the freedom but the responsibility to do that which the law prohibits.

We all live "under the law" to some degree. We are all subject to limitations that require that we take others into account as we go about our lives. Laws are good. They are necessary if we are to have a society that "works." They are meant to enhance our lives individually and collectively. But when we live only according to the "letter of the law," if we never allow ourselves to "step to the beat of a different drummer," our souls can become inhibited by what is prohibited, and we may become *less* rather than *more* alive.

Some of the greatest figures in history were free spirited when it came to the law; they gave themselves permission to act in ways that were prohibited. Jesus, Gandhi, Martin Luther King, and Dorothy Day among so many others, all responded to the needs of those they served by doing what was prohibited when a greater good was called for. They were not scofflaws; rather, they were being true to a "higher law," that of love, the inner imperative of their hearts – and of ours.

In less dramatic ways than those just mentioned, we are invited to make daily decisions in our interactions with one another. Do we do only what is permitted, only what is conventionally acceptable, only what fits within the confines of the culture? Or do we dare to give ourselves permission to do what is prohibited, to live above rather than under the law – that is to "walk the extra mile," to be foolishly, prodigally, lavishly loving when doing less is all that is expected or considered sufficient?

COSMIC LOTTERY

"So – true story – I'm walking down Jefferson Blvd. and this old, long gray-haired hippie dude … leaps out of the bushes and grabs me by the lapels … and he shouts at me, "You won! You won, my friend! You won!" … I said, "What did I win?" The old man cackled, "Hah! Don't you know?! You won the Cosmic Lottery!" "Cosmic lottery? Uhhhh … I don't recall buying a ticket for that one" I said … "Yes! Yes! That's it! The Cosmic Lottery: None of THIS had to be, yet it is! YOU didn't have to be, yet you are! You won!" … "All you have to do to collect is recognize how much it's worth, and then give it all away."

– John Monczunski[3]

It's not your everyday encounter writer John Monczunski relates in the above Facebook post. Being confronted by a wild man shouting what appears to be nonsense, but what may also be understood as a prophetic utterance is indeed a rare experience. We are not likely to be accosted by a deranged stranger, but hopefully we will somehow be made aware that we, too, without realizing our good fortune, have won the Cosmic Lottery that is life.

"None of THIS had to be, yet it is! YOU didn't have to be, yet you are!" How amazing is it to be alive, and to be the person we happen to be? Whether you believe in creationism or evolution, reality – even with all its imperfections, is pretty sacred stuff. We have won, we are here, we're alive, we are!

The old hippie topped off his "you won" declaration with this piece of wisdom: "All you have to do to collect is recognize how much it's worth, and then give it all away." Seems simple enough, but simple can be difficult. We don't win by collecting our winnings. We don't make the most of life by striving for and achieving material success and then pocketing our hard-earned wealth. We cash in on our winnings when we realize the value of life – its significance, its sacredness, its mystery. We win when we are open to the wonder of it all. And we "give it all away" when – by how fully we live and how compassionately we care – we share with others our appreciation and excitement for having "won."

The paradox at play here is that we always get more than we give. For every act of kindness, for every word of encouragement, every time we speak or act on behalf of the lost, the least, and the last, we receive a hundred-fold in return. We have indeed won the Cosmic Lottery. Now the challenge is to live it, and to give it all away.

CURVE YOUR STRAIGHT

Curve your straight
Widen your narrow
Don't crouch in a gully
Sample the peaks
Down in the dumps
your doom is secure
Resuscitate your ardor
Heat up your pizzazz
Put roller skates
on your pussy feet
Welcome the peril
of passionate dismay.
– James Broughton[4]

Have you ever felt that your life is small? Have you allowed yourself to be defined by your roles and responsibilities in a way that is confining? Have you wondered what it would be like to be more free and alive? My guess is that poet James Broughton has felt all of those things at times and that he penned the above poem to encourage himself and to invite us to live with a greater sense of joy, vitality, and at least a touch of pizzazz.

It is no easy task to remain young-at-heart as we assume the responsibilities that come with adulthood – earning a living, paying our bills, caring for those in our charge, providing for unexpected setbacks and for our inevitable decline. But the familiarity and repetition that often come with the territory of being accountable and dependable in our work and personal lives can cause us to lose touch with the fact that human beings are spiritual beings, and that being spiritual is about being fully alive.

It's been said that the difference between a rut and a grave are the dimensions! When Broughton claims that "down in the dumps your doom is secure," he is naming the truth that there can be a deadly sense of comfort when our daily routines become patterns that devolve into ruts. The proverbial "straight and narrow" is not a bad way to live, but its predictability can have a deadening effect on our soul.

What to do if we've lost our taste for "passionate dismay"? How can we resuscitate our ardour? What might it mean to put on roller skates? A more vibrant life is not necessarily a different life, but a different way to live life. It is about giving ourselves permission to try something new, to take risks, to think and to live "outside the box," to have the courage, in the words of Henry David Thoreau, to "step to the music of a different drummer" – one whose cadence is the tempo of the Spirit.

ELUSIVE HAPPINESS

As you know … I am talking about my life: my cushy, privileged, nicer-than-most life. I have almost exactly the life I always said I wanted, and I don't really like it very much. My creature comforts are adequate – more than adequate. I could use the same word for my friends. Then, too, there's the arena of professional accomplishment in which I am, well, accomplished. The point is that my life is stuffed to the gills with people, places, and things that ought to make me happy but they don't.

– Julia Cameron[5]

In her book *Prayers from a Nonbeliever*, artist and author Julia Cameron is not complaining about her life, about the fact that she isn't happy despite having a cushy existence; she's just being a bit perplexed and painfully honest about that reality. It can be hard to admit being discontent when we have so much when so many other people have so little, but it is not uncommon to feel empty in the midst of plenty, to experience a hunger that nothing or no one can satisfy.

Another person who experienced an inner-void despite being content with her life was Catholic Worker founder Dorothy Day, who wrote, "I meant a spiritual hunger … a loneliness that was in me no matter how happy I was and how fulfilled in my personal life." Day puts her finger on the *dis-ease* that sometimes afflicts us out of nowhere, a "loneliness" that breaks through when our guard is down – something's not right in the middle of the night.

It is not possible to be fully content or satisfied for long by "creature comforts" or by "professional accomplishment." True happiness eludes us when we attempt to grasp the things we believe will bring it about, for it is not something we can attain through attainments. Happiness is a byproduct of love, and love is the willingness to respond to the needs of others.

Because we are spiritual beings who share a common bond with all people, true happiness does not arise in isolation from others, but in communion with them. Greek playwright Sophocles knew this to be true when, five centuries before Christ, he posed the question, "Tell me. Given the choice, which would you prefer: happiness while your friends are in pain or to share in their suffering?"

HEART OVER HEAD

Love anything and your heart will be wrung and possibly broken. If you want to make sure of keeping it intact you must give it to no one, not even an animal. Wrap it carefully round with hobbies and little luxuries; avoid all entanglements. Lock it up safe in the casket or coffin of your selfishness, but in that casket, safe, dark, motionless, airless, it will change. It will not be broken; it will become unbreakable, impenetrable, irredeemable. To love is to be vulnerable.

– C. S. Lewis[6]

In this excerpt from his book *The Four Loves*, literary legend C. S. Lewis is not only talking about protecting ourselves from the pain of loss and disappointment inherent in relationships, romantic or otherwise, but about the heartbreak that can come when we open ourselves to all of life. If we "wrap it carefully round," we may escape heartache, but we will never experience the joy that can come from loving the simple things of life.

In his opus entitled "Aimless Love," poet Billy Collins writes about falling in love with, among other things, a wren, a dead mouse, a bowl of broth, a hot evening shower, and a bar of soap. It would seem that there is medication for such a one! It may be crazy to fall for such ordinary things, but it may also be crazy not to, for there is so much to be smitten by, so many things that can quicken our hearts. Our life is diminished if we are insensitive to the stunning significance of the ordinary.

What Lewis encourages and what Collins experiences is vulnerability to the common, everyday reality that is life in the world. When, in the same poem, Collins claims that, "my heart is always propped up in a field on its tripod, ready for the next arrow,"[7] he is saying that he's ready and willing to be wounded by the simple beauty that surrounds us and that is present even in those things and people that may not be beautiful.

Allowing ourselves to fall in love with life is not a matter of being "head over heels," but of being "heart over head." The former is infatuation; it is runaway emotion while the latter is an honouring of emotion, the choice to lead with our heart rather than protect it. Living in this fashion will surely result in heartbreak from time to time, but this is a small price to pay for the joy of being fully alive.

I HAVE A DREAM

I have a dream. It is a dream deeply rooted in the American dream.

I have a dream that one day this nation will rise up and live out the true meaning of its creed: "We hold these truths to be self-evident: that all men are created equal."

I have a dream that … the sons of former slaves and the sons of former slave owners will be able to sit down together at the table of brotherhood …

I have a dream that my four little children will one day live in a nation where they will not be judged by the color of their skin but by the content of their character ...

I have a dream that one day ... little black boys and black girls will be able to join hands with little white boys and white girls and walk together as sisters and brothers.

I have a dream ...

– Dr. Martin Luther King, Jr.

Delivered on the steps of the Lincoln Memorial on August 28, 1963, Martin Luther King, Jr.'s "I Have a Dream" speech ranks in greatness to Lincoln's Gettysburg Address, and Franklin D. Roosevelt's "Infamy Speech," presented on the day following Japan's attack on Pearl Harbor.

Dr. King's dream was not only a vision, a hope, and a possibility. It was not merely a pipe dream, for it was also a task – one that required the willingness to spend his life, and ultimately to give his life. His was a dream about equality, freedom from oppression, and the recognition that even those who oppose us are our sisters and brothers. What Dr. King modelled for us in the face of the hateful reaction to his message was expressed in his saying, *"Whom you would change, you must first love."*

Those who find comfort in homogeneity do not look upon this kind of dream kindly. For them, diversity is a threat rather than a reality that adds to the beauty of the mosaic that is humanity. Dr King's dream challenges us to look closely at ourselves and at our sometimes-subtle attitudes and outlooks that contribute to a world at odds. If we dig beneath the rubble of our judgments, stereotypes, insecurities, and fears, we may find that our thinking about differences – political, racial, religious, gender, sexual orientation and the like – do not align with the person we would like to be.

French poet Paul Valery says the best way to make your dreams come true is to wake up! So, too, the best way to make our daydreams come to fruition is to "get up." Whether our dreams are in the socio-political, professional, or personal arenas of life, we can right our wrongs and make improvements only if we are up to the challenge of acknowledging and confronting our unconscious prejudices.

IN SYNC WITH THE SACRED

We live in a culture that begs us to conform. Through its various messages, it calls us to squeeze into its mold. It exerts external pressure on our minds to believe in and buy its opinions, hopes, and aspirations. Yet, the pursuits that define most of our culture never fully satisfy our heart and soul …

In response, the world will tell us to just run faster, reach farther, work harder, make more, and become conformed more deeply. But its promised offer of fulfillment always remains out of reach. Our deepest longings are left unsatisfied.

— Joshua Becker[8]

The words above come from motivational speaker Joshua Becker whose message is one of living an authentic life. I have found that living in this manner involves being in sync with something sacred – an intuition; a sixth sense; a deep, voiceless voice that summons us beyond the conventional wisdom of society, those ways of thinking, believing, and behaving that go unquestioned. The values society espouses, "run faster, reach farther, work harder, make more" are not necessarily misguided, it's just that, because we are spiritual beings, we can never experience fulfillment by living in this way.

When we live in accord with the conventions of society, when we fit in, we gain the approval of the group, or at least we do not experience its disapproval. Living within the confines of convention satisfies important needs for belonging and acceptance, but the sacred within does not invite us to fit in. Rather, it summons us to stand out.

When living in sync with the sacred becomes our *modus operandi*, we are likely to find ourselves out of step with most others, for the dictates that emanate from within challenge us to embrace paradox (loosely interpreted as crooked teaching). These are gospel-like ways of living based on beliefs such as the last shall be first, the greatest serve the rest, and that we are most alive when we die to ourselves (put the needs of others before our own preferences).

Authentic living is not about being a rebel or a nonconformist, it is about something much more radical – namely, being faithful to the deepest dimension of ourselves, in sync with the presence of the Sacred within.

INTERDEPENDENCE DAY

One old Hasidic rabbi asked his pupils how they could tell when the night had ended and the day had begun, for that is the time for certain holy prayers. "Is it," proposed one student, "when you can see an animal in the distance and tell whether it is a sheep or a dog?" "No," answered the rabbi. "Is it when you can clearly see the lines on your own palm?" "Is it when you can look at a tree in the distance and tell if it is a fig or a pear tree?" "No," answered the rabbi each time. "Then what is it?" the pupils demanded. "It is when you can look on the face of any man or woman and see that they are your sister or brother. Until then it is still night."

– Jack Kornfield[9]

This story speaks to the heart of our connection with all people. Just because we do not know another person does not mean we are strangers. Just because we have differences and disagreements between us does not mean we cannot be friends. And just because our language, the colour of our skin, our religion, or our sexual orientation differs, does not mean we are unrelated

Resisting the impulse to make enemies out of people who look, think, or believe differently from us is often difficult, for diversity can feel like a threat to the comfort and security we seek – usually unconsciously – in homogeneous groups. But we are citizens of the world before we are citizens of any country; we belong to God, by whatever name, before we belong to any particular faith family.

Huston Smith, an authority on comparative religions, offers good advice in this matter when he says, "Beware of the differences that blind us to the unity that binds us." The celebration of Independence Day is an opportunity to realize that our self-reliance, both as individuals and as a nation, can keep us from recognizing that we are all sisters and brothers. Despite our differences, *we are essentially interdependent.*

The notion of interdependence brings to mind an African proverb: "If you want to go fast, go alone; if you want to go far, go together." There is much to be said for the ability to stand on one's own, but we need each other if we are to go far in becoming our best personally, interpersonally, and internationally. The awareness that we are interdependent challenges us to relate to each other in ways that build bridges, not walls.

Every morning the sunrise brings an end to night, but darkness will remain upon the earth so long as we allow our ethnic, religious, philosophical, and political differences to overshadow the common spiritual bond that unites us.

JUST PASSING THROUGH

We live in the most affluent culture the world has ever seen. Estimates are that although we have only 6 percent of the world's population in America, we use almost half of the natural resources. It seems to me that if more were actually better, we would live in the happiest, most satisfied culture of all time. But we don't. Not even close. In fact, we live in one of the most dissatisfied cultures on record.

It's not that having a lot of things is bad, wrong, or harmful in and of itself, only that the desire to have more and more and more is insatiable. As long as you think more is better, you'll never be satisfied.

— Richard Carlson[10]

Conventional wisdom is any assumption that is believed to be unquestionably true and universally accepted. In our First World culture, "busy is good," "more is better," and "success equals wealth," are examples. As author Richard Carlson claims, there is nothing inherently "bad, wrong, or harmful" with affluence, it's just that once we succumb to the glitter of more is better, it can feel like there's never enough.

Minister and social activist William Sloane Coffin has opined that *there are two ways to be rich: one is to have a lot of money, the other is to have fewer needs.* What he didn't say is how to achieve this less-is-better attitude. It becomes possible to be satisfied with less when we are in touch with our soul, that deep, sacred self that knows intuitively that fewer needs and fewer belongings are the portal to true happiness and deep peace.

Because material possessions are necessary for our survival, dealing with our "dark side" in relation to an abundance of them becomes a delicate dance. Yes, we can become possessed by our possessions, but we cannot do without them either. How an awareness of impermanence can enable us to negotiate this dance is the lesson in the following story. A spiritual seeker, having heard about a hermit of great wisdom, found his way to the wise man's dwelling. Upon entering he was struck by its sparse furnishings – two chairs, a bed, and a table. He asked the hermit, "Where is your furniture?"

The hermit replied, "Where is yours?"

"I have none," said the seeker. "I'm just passing through."

"So am I," the hermit responded.

We're all "just passing through." We are all here for a short time. We are all under the influence of affluence. But if we fall prey to the allure of "more is better," our passing through can become much more cumbersome materially, and burdensome spiritually.

LIFE IS SHORT

Life is short. Remember that, too. I've always known this. Or almost always. I've been living with mortality for decades, since my mother died of ovarian cancer when she was forty and I was nineteen. And this is what I learned from that experience: that knowledge of our own mortality is the greatest gift God ever gives us.

It is so easy to waste our lives: our days, our hours, our minutes ... It is so easy to exist instead of live unless you know there is a clock ticking. So many of us changed our lives when we heard a biological clock and decided to have kids. But that sound is a murmur compared to the tolling of mortality.

– Anna Quindlen[11]

These sobering words written as a commencement address by novelist and columnist Anna Quindlen are not the typical "go out and get 'em, set the world on fire" speech college graduates expect. After all, most grads are at the peak of their lives physically – the reality of mortality is likely the farthest thing from their minds.

By focusing on the inevitability of death, Quindlen is attempting to communicate a message about life. "It is so easy to exist instead of live," she says. It is so easy to fall into habits that become patterns that become ruts. Unless we are vigilant, we become lulled and dulled by what is familiar and can come to the end of our day – and days – wondering whether we have truly lived.

Ours is a death-denying culture. It's considered morbid to think or talk about dying. But it is important to be aware of our impermanence, for unless "there is a clock ticking," and there always is, we are likely to take the gift of life for granted. What an amazing thing it is to walk and talk; to drive a car and ride a bike; to see, hear, taste, smell, and feel the textures of life on planet earth. Every day, even the difficult ones, is a miracle unfolding before us, but we're mostly too "asleep" to notice. Thank God for our pets and young children who remind us to marvel at what just is.

Every morning is a commencement wherein we venture forth into the world. Every day is filled with possibilities beyond our imagining. Yes, we are likely to repeat patterns of behaviour that are predictable, but even these can have an element of newness to them if we approach them with a fresh mind and heart.

The fact that you are not dead is not sufficient proof that you are alive! If you are reading this, you are not dead, but the question remains – are you as alive as you can be?

ONE-PIECE PUZZLE

Let us train ourselves to desire what the situation demands.
– Seneca

A puzzle is interesting and engaging because it is made up of many pieces different in shape, size, and colour. There is no such thing as a one-piece puzzle. Because it is a multi-faceted affair, the same could be said of life. Life is full of joys and sorrows, work and play, people and activities, some of which we find interesting and others boring, some pleasurable and some painful. And like a puzzle, every odd-shaped, perplexing piece of life belongs – each contributes to making the finished product. Life is anything but a one-piece puzzle.

Most of us are pretty responsible. We do not refuse to perform the sometimes-difficult tasks that come with our roles at work, within our families, or in the broader community. We may procrastinate when it comes to doing what we dislike, but eventually we roll up our sleeves and get the job done. There is, however, a difference between performing difficult tasks and embracing them. When we fail to *willingly* engage those aspects of our life we find distasteful, life can become a chore – a burden rather than a blessing – and we become both tired and resentful.

We always have before us the choice between burden and blessing. Each day is filled not only with situations and relationships we take delight in, but also those that drain us. How we deal with the "tough stuff" makes all the difference. The Roman sage Seneca once said, "Let us train ourselves to *desire* what the situation demands." If we take his wise words to heart, every annoying person, every odious task, every frustrating interruption, everything we wish we could wish away, can be considered pieces of a puzzle without which our life would not only be less interesting, but less complete.

PEACE THAT SURPASSES UNDERSTANDING

We have to fight them daily, like fleas, those many small worries about the morrow, for they sap our energies. We make mental provision for the days to come and everything turns out differently, quite differently … The things that have to be done must be done, and for the rest we must not allow ourselves to become infested with thousands of petty fears and worries, so many motions of no confidence in God. Ultimately, we have just one moral duty; to reclaim large areas of peace in ourselves, more and more peace and to reflect it towards others. And the more peace there is in us, the more peace there will also be in our troubled world.

– Etty Hillesum[12]

As with most everything of real importance, it's easier said than done when it comes to keeping ourselves from becoming "infested with thousands of petty fears and worries." Most of us are susceptible to being kidnapped from the present by the many cares and concerns that intrude on our minds and hearts. Although our fears and worries are often well-founded, when we give them the power to distract us it is difficult to stay focused on the here and now, and impossible to remain at peace.

Etty Hillesum, the author of the above quote, was not immune from fears and worries, and she knew what it meant to live in a "troubled world." Etty, a Dutch Jew, did not survive the Holocaust, but she did manage to remain at peace despite the unimaginable horrors through which she lived.

In this passage from her diary, Etty reminds herself, and us, that our first moral duty is to protect and promote inner peace, and she rightly claims that doing so can have a powerful impact on others and on the world.

If Etty is right in saying that petty fears and worries are "motions of no confidence in God," then maintaining inner peace is not merely a matter of learning how to fend off "worries about the morrow." Rather, it is about having faith that no matter what happens, there is a larger, sacred reality in which everything unfolds. Etty knew that she and her family and friends would not survive the death camps, but she never lost the sense that both life and death are dimensions of a mystery beyond comprehension. Inner peace, for Etty, was a byproduct of this conviction.

We probably all make "mental provision for the days to come." We all expect that there will be a tomorrow, and we have hopes and dreams about what it will look like. True peace comes when we hold those hopes lightly and when we trust that even if our fears and worries should come to pass, there is a peace that surpasses understanding.

READY OR NOT

Life always gives us exactly the teacher we need at every moment. This includes every mosquito, every misfortune, every red light, every traffic jam, every obnoxious superior (or employee), every illness, every loss, every moment of joy or depression, every addiction, every piece of junk, every breath. Every moment is the guru.

— Charlotte Joko Beck[13]

Perhaps you've heard the saying, "When the student is ready the teacher will come." According to author Charlotte Joko

Beck, the teacher is always present – ready or not. Giving her the benefit of the doubt may be difficult. Come on! Mosquitoes, traffic jams, people that get on our nerves … ? But to reject her wisdom means that we would spend much of our time and energy resisting life instead of learning its many lessons.

Presuming you agree that rejecting our teachers is not a good way to use the little time we have on this earth, the question becomes what are we to learn from them, and why are we so often reluctant to learn it? Could the lesson be that we don't really have much control over what happens? But we already know that. Could it be that what doesn't kill us will make us stronger? But we know that, too. Perhaps what we are to learn is that every aspect of life, especially the most trying, can by our openness to them be the entrée to a spiritual depth we didn't know we had, one that can sustain us in the midst of trials. Not a fun lesson, but one that can serve us well.

And why are we, generally speaking, reluctant learners? The word "stubborn" comes to mind! I know I tend to dig in my heels when life is other than what I prefer. Rather than being willing to accept and deal with what is difficult and distasteful, I resist and resent before it occurs to me that I may benefit from what is happening. Better a slow-learner than a dufus!

Life is full of annoying, hurtful, and harmful events and people. It seems counterintuitive, if not masochistic, to view this reality as something positive, something that could benefit us, something we would do well to embrace rather than reject. But if everything and everyone can be our teacher, and if we value learning and growing, then living with a mind and heart open to all that life brings our way may not be as masochistic as it seems.

SHHH ...

Go placidly amid the noise and haste,
and remember what peace there may be in silence.
– Max Ehrmann

I think 99 times and find nothing. I stop thinking,
swim in the silence, and the truth comes to me.
– Albert Einstein

Silence is the language of God, everything else
is poor translation.
– Rumi

My life is noisy but my being is silent.
– Thomas Merton

There is within each of us a still point surrounded by silence.
– Dag Hammarskjöld

Be still and know that I am God.
– Psalm 46:10

A poet, a theoretical physicist, a Muslim mystic, a Catholic monk, a Swedish diplomat, and a psalmist, all sing the praises of silence and its cousin stillness. There must be something to them! Silence and stillness are rare commodities in our noisy, fast-paced culture. They can seem like a refusal to use the ability to speak and act. Being still can be thought a form of laziness, and though we may take a moment of silence to honour a person who has died or to acknowledge an over-whelming situation, many of us are more likely to use words like "awkward," "oppressive," or even "deadly" to describe our experience of silence.

The ability to speak and act are surely things for which to be grateful, as they make communication and accomplishments possible. But when our lives are devoid of silence and stillness, when we are constantly surrounded by noise and immersed in busyness, we tend to lose touch with our souls – a loss whose ripple effect can result in our being strangers to ourselves and estranged from others. In his book *The Power of Silence*, Graham Turner writes the following.

In the hurly-burly of doing, all the frenetic activity, we don't do much reflecting and listening, we find it difficult to switch off to see what is really happening in our lives. It's as if we were running ourselves like companies, but never doing an audit.

Silence gives you a much better chance of hearing yourself, of being in touch with both your conscience and your demons ... [14]

As is the case in the business world, audits of a personal nature are not usually any fun. When we stop to take stock of ourselves, we may see not only light, but darkness as well – our fears, shame, guilt, insecurity, and the like. It takes courage to look closely at the person we are, but the payoff is worth the pain. Then silent stillness is not awkward, oppressive, or deadly, not something to fear, but more like the peaceful calm of a snowy winter evening – "Silent night, holy night ... "

SUCCESS

A few years ago, a man who was compiling a book entitled Success wrote and asked me to contribute a statement on how I had got to be a success. I replied indignantly that I was not allowed to consider myself a success ... If it so happened that I had once written a best seller, this was a pure accident ... and I would take very good care never to do the same again …

If I had a message for my contemporaries it is surely this:
Be anything you like, be madmen, drunks, and bastards of
every shape and form, but at all costs avoid one thing: success.
If you are too obsessed with success, you will forget to live …

– Thomas Merton[15]

Never one to mince words, monk, mystic, and social critic Thomas Merton reacted strongly to the suggestion that he could be considered a success. Though he lived in the cloistered seclusion of a monastery, Merton's prominence as a writer – his autobiography *The Seven Storey Mountain* has sold millions – made him a household name in the mid-20th century. But fame and fortune, usually thought to be indicators of success, were of no interest to him, for he had chosen to measure his worth by a different standard.

Merton's message for his contemporaries and for us is one of contradiction, which literally means "against the word." Every society has its "word," its message, its definition of success, which is usually based on wealth, power, position, and the like. We "climb the ladder," get a raise, accomplish our goals, garner the praise of others. Nothing wrong with any of this, but it leaves little room for failure! Yes, failure. Failure is thought to be the opposite of success but is really central to it according to Winston Churchill, who once opined that success consists of going from failure to failure without loss of enthusiasm. Success, in other words, is a matter of character; it is not about unimpeded achievement, but about who we become when the going gets tough.

Success is not a goal to achieve, but is, according to writer Bessie Stanley, the result of having "lived well, laughed often, and loved much … " It is, she says, the entitlement of "he who has left the world better than he found it." Despite his objection to it, perhaps Merton was a success after all. And despite the fact that we may never be wealthy or famous, we, too, might claim that distinction.

SWAMPLANDS OF THE SOUL

[S]ooner or later, all of us are ushered by fate, by the actions of others, by choices we make, both conscious and unconscious, into places we do not wish to visit. Such rooms in our common psychic mansion we label depression, loss, grief, addiction, anxiety, envy, shame, and the like ... In these dismal environs we are flooded by anxiety because the fact of being out of control is no longer deniable. Accordingly, and typically, we tend to kick into our former management systems – denial, projection onto others, addiction, frenetic activity – and we mire deeper and deeper in the swamp.

– James Hollis[16]

How's that for a cheery start to a reflection! In his book *What Matters Most*, Jungian analyst James Hollis ventures into our "dismal environs" in an attempt to name and claim the fact that no one escapes the inevitability of soul-searing times. Try as we might to outrun them, the likes of depression, loss, and grief will eventually catch up to us. Hollis intimates that a better tactic would be to adopt the wisdom of philosopher Ralph Waldo Emerson, who said that if a dog is chasing you, stop and whistle for it!

The reason it is wise to embrace "such rooms in our common psychic mansion" is that by doing so we open the door to our soul. It's been said that religious people *believe* in hell; spiritual people have *been there*. When we face what we fear, we not only take away much of its power, but we also come to realize that we have the capacity to prevail. There is within us a Presence and Power waiting to be discovered.

Anne Lamott is not only an author, but a person who knows what it is like to face her demons. She refers to that Presence and Power when she states that courage is fear that has said its prayers. The courage to face what frightens us does not dispel fear, but opening ourselves to a Higher/Inner Power enables us to move through our fear and to enter with confidence "places we do not wish to visit."

Buddhists say that when you walk into the fire, you find out it's raining in there! Nothing is as bad as it seems from the outside, but we have to enter the swamplands of the soul in order to experience this.

TAKE THE WHOLE KIT

Take the whole kit
with the caboodle
Experience life
don't deplore it
Shake hands with time
don't kill it
Open a lookout
Dance on a brink
Run with your wildfire
You are closer to glory
Leaping an abyss
than upholstering a rut
– James Broughton[17]

Poet James Broughton encourages us to take the whole kit with the caboodle; to be open to the pain and the pleasure, the hard and the easy, the difficult and the delightful, the yin and the yang of life. Sounds counterintuitive if you ask me, and maybe even a little masochistic, like risking harm is as desirable as playing it safe. But the poet insists on singing the praises of peril by inviting us to take chances, to explore new territory, to confront our fears, even if the outcome of doing so could be our undoing.

The aversion to flirting with danger notwithstanding, we know there is wisdom in the saying "no pain no gain." Everything from muscles to memory to mettle must be pushed to their limits if we are to become our best selves. We can spend our days "upholstering a rut," but if we do, we are likely to come to the end of our days regretting that we did not live more fully, that we did not take chances while we had the chance. The "caboodle" of comfort, security, caution, and predictability have an important place in life, but kit and caboodle are partners, they are bundled, it's a package deal.

Try as we might, we cannot outrun danger, for it is part of the fabric of life. We can, however, be willing to face danger by making changes, taking on new challenges, and choosing to wander outside our comfort zone. In the poet's words, we can "shake hands with time," "dance on a brink," "run with our wildfire," "leap an abyss." When we live in this manner, he says, we are "closer to glory," closer to participating in the sacred, God-energy that is life.

THE ROAD NOT TAKEN

Poet Robert Frost was awaiting admittance ... into a student fraternity and was told confidentially that only one factor was delaying his entry: the fact that he took long walks in the woods by himself ... He was caught being an individual, with an inner life of his own, instead of the dead and public machine life of joining a crowd ... When they asked him what he did while

walking alone in the woods, he was not so foolish as to admit
the truth that he was guilty of writing poetry there. Instead, he
saved the day and won his fraternity acceptance by replying:
"Gnawing the bark off trees."

– Peter Viereck[18]

Robert Frost was born in the latter part of the 19th century, but it appears to be the case that even in what may seem to us a simpler era than our own, a person who felt the need to spend time alone was considered odd. For Frost, and for many others, alone time is essential for creativity, emotional and physical renewal, and for connecting with soul. I'm not aware of their being such a thing as a "spiritual Fitbit," but if there were it might measure the fact that taking long, slow, solitary walks to nowhere is a particularly good way to nurture our spiritual health.

Frost was "caught being an individual, with an inner life of his own." Though he wanted to gain entry into a fraternity and thus was aware of his need for community, he valued spending long hours in nature by himself. There is a gravitational pull, a conventional wisdom, a societal ethos that calls us to join in, to think like, and to shape our lives by our culture's standards. Although there can be good in this, without soul time we are apt to lose touch with the sacred depth that is the place of the divine within.

It's been said that the superior person understands what is right, while the inferior one understands what will sell! It is important to be practical and reasonable, but it is essential to be spiritual, for without a sense for this dimension of our self, we run the risk of being strangers to ourselves and estranged from meaningful relationships with others. Being spiritual is not about rising above and beyond the practical, but about going deep within it. When we are down-to-earth, when we are sensually present to life, when we give ourselves room to reflect and not just analyze, we are close to that which makes us the unique individuals we are.

In what is arguably his most famous poem, "The Road Not Taken," Frost writes, "Two roads diverged in a wood, and I – I took the one less traveled by, and that has made all the difference." We don't have to walk in the woods to connect with our soul, but if we are to be our best self we may at times have to take a road less travelled – one characterized by quiet, solitude, and reflection – lest we fall prey to the "dead public machine life."

THE VIRTUE OF EMPTINESS

Early Christian monks went out to live in the desert in order to find emptiness. Modern life is becoming so full that we need our ways of going to the desert to be relieved of our plenty. Our heads are crammed with information, our lives busy with activities, our cities stuffed with automobiles, our imaginations bloated on pictures and images ... our homes cluttered with gadgets, and conveniences. We honor productivity to such an extent that the unproductive person or day seems a failure.
– Thomas Moore[19]

Psychotherapist, author, and former monk Thomas Moore holds that in our culture it verges on the sacrilegious to claim that less is more, that slow may be preferable to fast, or that doing nothing can be time well spent. We seem to have made a religion out of information, accumulation, and acceleration. We worship at the altar of productivity and fullness and have lost any appreciation for the value and virtue of emptiness – the spaciousness our souls require like our bodies require air.

It has been said that nature abhors a vacuum and so it seems does human nature. We fill the void of silence with noise, the void of inactivity with busyness, and the void of simplicity with more things than we need. Having fallen prey to the culture's dictate that more is better, we would do well to heed the message offered by minister and peace activist William Sloane Coffin who stated that there are two ways to be rich: one is to have a lot of money and the other is to have fewer needs.

There can be a great deal of beauty in deserts, but as a metaphor they usually symbolize those times in life when we experience dryness and difficulty, struggle and hardship. Deserts of this sort are "places" from which we would rather escape than linger. But if we value the life of our soul, if we learn from the example of monks and others who recognize the importance of emptiness, we come to realize that desert experiences can be times of quiet, inner peace when we reprioritize where we put our energy, and where we can get back to the basics of living a simple life, one devoid of the fullness that does not satisfy.

The wisdom of living a simple life is beneficial not only for each of us, but for all of us, a truth reflected in the saying "live simply so others can simply live." Despite differences and distances ethnically, religiously, politically, and geographically, we are connected to one another. How we choose to live impacts both the planet and its people.

TRUE HEALING

Most people have come to prefer certain of life's experiences and deny and reject others, unaware of the value of the hidden things that may come wrapped in plain or even ugly paper. In avoiding all pain and seeking comfort at all cost, we may be left

without intimacy or compassion; in rejecting change and risk
we often cheat ourselves of the quest; in denying our suffering
we may never know our strength or our greatness …

It is natural, even instinctive to prefer comfort to pain, the
familiar to the unknown. But sometimes our instincts are not
wise. Life usually offers us far more than our biases and
preferences will allow us to have. Beyond comfort lie grace,
mystery, and adventure.

– Rachel Remen, MD[20]

The above was penned by someone who knows what she's talking about. Rachel Remen MD, is both physician and patient, having suffered from Crohn's disease most of her life. While treating countless patients and enduring her own physical and emotional pain, Remen has come to realize the importance of engaging the soul in the healing process. This, of course, is wise counsel not only in the medical profession but in all of life, and not only in dealing with others but in relation to ourselves as well.

Healing is not about mending what is broken or relieving what is painful, for this is more a matter of curing. Healing refers to identifying and moving beyond impediments to wholeness, growth, and achieving our potential as human beings. Healing is a matter of being in touch with our soul, the presence of the divine in us.

"No pain, no gain" is an adage used by those engaged in strength training, where building muscle and increasing strength require going beyond what one can do comfortably. This statement is true not only physically but also when growth is valued mentally, emotionally, socially, and spiritually. It may be counterintuitive to go beyond comfort and familiarity in every dimension of life, but this is what is required if we are to experience healing.

"In rejecting change and risk, we often cheat ourselves of the quest." When we embrace life as a quest to connect with our soul rather than as an accumulation of years during which we seek only to achieve goals of material, financial, and relational comfort and security, we may begin to sense a sacred restlessness. This is not necessarily an indication that we should make drastic changes like quitting our job or leaving home and family behind, but it is an invitation to open ourselves to the unknown.

Without realizing it, we spend every day walking on thin ice. Comfort, familiarity, and practicality can keep us from breaking through to an awareness of the "grace, mystery, and adventure" that lie just beneath the surface of the life we are living.

WORLD HOUSE

In an essay published shortly before his death, Martin Luther King, Jr., wrote of the dangers of closed tribes as the "great new problem of mankind":

"We have inherited a large house, a great 'world house' in which we have to live together – black and white, Easterner and Westerner, Gentile and Jew, Catholic and Protestant, Moslem and Hindu – a family unduly separated in ideas, culture and interest, who, because we can never again live apart, must learn somehow to live with each other in peace."

He went on to say that all inhabitants of the globe are now neighbors; "all men are interdependent" and "all life is interrelated."

– Diana Butler-Bass[21]

The word "neighbour" comes from the Old English word *neahgebur*, which means "near-dweller." By this definition, a neighbour can literally be anyone who lives in our geographical vicinity. The word neighbour may also refer to a person we know and who knows us, someone with whom we are familiar even from afar.

Although familiarity is more personal than someone who happens to live next door, down the block, or in the same building as us, it is not the most profound meaning of "neighbour." When Jesus was asked "Who is my neighbor?" (Luke 10:29), he responded by telling the parable of the Good Samaritan, a story that, along with being a radical indictment of the religious elite (speaking truth to power), makes the point that a true neighbour is a person who responds to the plight of one in need, who gives hands-on care even to a stranger. And when Dr. King says, "all inhabitants of the globe are now neighbors," he too is being prophetic by positing that each one of us has a responsibility to attend to others, no matter where they live or what our differences.

Religious scholar and author Huston Smith cautions us to "beware of the differences that blind us to the unity that binds us." Unity is not merely a matter of likeness. It is not about common ethnicity, religion, economic status, sexual orientation, political persuasion, and the like, for these are very real differences. When we identify with them, such groupings can make us "closed tribes"; they become not just the substance of differences, but the source of divisions. The unity that binds us has to do with our spiritual essence, with the fact that what enlivens all of us is the same – we share a common source and sustaining force.

We live in a global village, the earth is our "hood," our planet is a "world house." Because we live under the same celestial ceiling, because the ground upon which we walk is our shared floor, we are neighbours, yes, but housemates, too, called not merely to get along, but to realize that we belong to each other.

TWO

RESISTING THE PULL OF PERFECTIONISM

Airbrushed Airheads
Backwards/Forwards
Cut Yourself Some Slack
Drop the Struggle
Enter Grace
Every Person Is Worthwhile
Holy Fools
In Defence of Ruins
In Praise of Stumbling
Laughing at Our Folly
Loving Our Imperfect Selves
Mistakes and Forgiveness
Ode to Joy
Pure Prayer
Sincerely Yours
Stumbling Blocks or Building Blocks
The Crooked Path Home
The Master Limps
To Err Is Human
Torn to Pieces

THE HEAVY SCENT OF PER-
FECTION IS PRESENT IN THE AIR WE BREATHE. Rare is
the person who has not inhaled perfection's demanding
message nor has felt the heave and haul of its persistent
presence. The need to achieve perfection in our personal,
professional, and religious and spiritual lives often leaves us
discouraged at our failure to arrive at the too-difficult-to-
attain goal of being who we are, and of doing what we do
without fault or flaw.

It is when we lighten up, when we cut ourselves slack,
and when we look the monster of perfectionism in the eye
that we become free from its influence, despite its presence
at the door of our psyche. We do not defeat perfectionism
by resisting it but by refusing to answer when it knocks.

The reflections in this section sing the praises of imperfection, the "I'm good enough" wisdom that enables us to
be and to do our best without undue judgment and self-
criticism.

AIRBRUSHED AIRHEADS

*Here's a fact of life: Nobody gets away scot-free. In every life, we
are destined to find some disappointment, dissatisfaction, pain,
and illness. We are bound to feel confused, insecure, and anxious.*

*Regularly contemplating the travails of our journey helps
us to stay realistic about what life is and isn't ... Every dip and
rise, every twist and turn is part of the infinite journey; why
turn aside from any of it?*

Too many of us resist authenticity, preferring instead an airbrushed approach to the world … Too much airbrush reality on a daily basis and we become airheads.

– Surya Das[22]

"Nobody gets away scot-free" – now there's a happy thought! Appearances aside, author Surya Das opines that nobody is "livin' the dream," at least not for long. Why, he asks, turn aside from any of it, meaning the unwanted dips and twists. Maybe it's because we don't want to become morbid. Maybe we'd prefer to look on the bright side of life and, as the old song states, we'd rather direct our feet "to the sunny side of the street."

There is certainly something to say for focusing on the positive, for turning our gaze on those aspects of life for which we are grateful. But there is also good reason to be "realistic about what life is and isn't," and to not only look upon darker truths but to open ourselves to what they might have to teach us. Airbrushed reality may be more pleasant to consider, but it presents a perverted version of reality, one that can make it difficult for us to accept the unadorned truth about who we are, how we look, and what we have or have not achieved.

So what is the payoff in turning toward rather than away from life's harsh truths? Two things come to mind. One is that doing so can teach us that fear, when faced, is not as frightening as it seems. What we fear loses its power to intimidate when we take command of a situation, when we choose to engage rather than turn a blind eye to what is unappealing. Another life lesson might be that we have inner resources we may not realize until we venture outside our comfort zone, until, that is, we brush up against – rather than airbrush – what we find daunting. There is a spiritual strength and resilience we can bring to bear when we feel overwhelmed, a confidence that comes *through* us rather than *from* us.

It's true that nobody gets away scot-free, but it's also true that embracing this fact can be the catalyst that transforms us into people who are less fearful, and more confident – anything but airheads!

BACKWARDS/FORWARDS

I want to live my life backwards: You start out dead and get that out of the way. Then you wake up in a nursing home feeling better every day. Then you get kicked out for being too healthy. You enjoy your retirement and collect your pension. Then when you start work, you get a gold watch on your first day. You work forty years until you're too young to work. You get ready for (college) high school: drink alcohol, party. Then you go to primary school, you become a kid. You play, and you have no responsibilities. Then you become a baby and then …
you spend your last nine months floating peacefully in luxury, in spa-like conditions: central heating, room service on tap …

– George Carlin[23]

Sounds pretty good, eh? Comedian George Carlin is on to something when he suggests that life might be better if we lived it in reverse – get the tough stuff out of the way so we can have more fun the longer we're alive. The way it is now, we're always trying hard to become or remain looking and feeling young, which is a losing battle. And besides, the older we are the harder it is to blow out all those candles on our birthday cake!

As attractive as it may appear to live life backwards, that's not the cup of tea we have to drink. Danish philosopher Sørin Kierkegaard says life can only be understood backwards, but it must be lived forwards. In retrospect, we're all pretty wise. Looking back, we can see what we should have said or done. With hindsight, we know right from wrong, smart from foolish.

Despite baseball great Satchel Paige's warning not to look back because something might be gaining on us, it's important to revisit our lives from time to time in order to understand, learn, and grow through our mistakes lest we repeat them – which we sometimes do anyway! But living forward is the only right way to go.

Living forward implies the willingness to take risks, to forge new pathways, to believe in ourselves, and to have faith in the benevolence of life. Yes, we will make mistakes, we will fail, and we will face what appear to be insurmountable difficulties, but by opening ourselves to life we will ultimately achieve a simple kind of greatness – the fulfillment of our potential.

Humorist Dave Barry claims that we can only be young once, but we can always be immature! Living life backwards, trying to hang on to elusive youth and carefree happiness, can easily morph into immaturity. Better to move forward with a positive attitude that allows us to embrace what may come, like it or not.

CUT YOURSELF SOME SLACK

The road to enlightenment is long and difficult, and you should try not to forget snacks and magazines.
– Anne Lamott[24]

As we journey along the road of life, moving by fits and starts toward becoming who and how we want to be, it's good to cut ourselves some slack.

I have to laugh at myself when I realize how hard it is for me to practice what I preach. One of the things I enjoy most is travelling to different cities to give talks or lead retreats and workshops. More specifically, what I like is the opportunity to have the privacy and quiet seclusion of the hotel rooms in which I stay. I always look forward to this solitary time as a mini-retreat, and a time to accomplish work that is difficult to do in the midst of familiar surroundings and day-to-day demands. But what happens more often than not is that when I get to the room at the end of the day, I pick up the television remote and channel surf until I fall asleep! The next morning my initial instinct is to give myself a hard time for not following through with my more productive plans, but deeper down I know that along with snacks and a magazine, a few television shows have their place on the journey.

Anyone out there like me? Do any of you have big ideas about how best to use your time and energy, but when the opportunities present themselves you cave to some less lofty option? Despite our best intentions, many of us fall prey to what feels good in the moment instead of doing what would feel good if we accomplished it. Everything from housework to homework, from what I *should* do to what I *have* to do can take second place to the appeal of chill.

I'm grateful to have come across the notion that "snacks and magazines" can be a good idea as we strive to accomplish our goals, for my inclination is to soldier on until the job gets done. This approach to life can be productive, but it can also lead to burnout and resentment. Whether the goals we strive for are spiritual or material, personal or professional, the better way to progress when possible is to cut ourselves some slack.

Downtime can be good time. Time out can be time well

spent. Taking a break can prevent us from having a breakdown. We are people, not machines. We need to honour our limits as well as exceed them from time to time. Arriving at our destination depleted is not necessarily something to brag about, as it may be an indication that we don't have the common sense to care for ourselves.

Because for many of us enlightenment and senility are in a race to the finish line, it can feel like time is running out and that taking a break is not advisable. But as Aesop's fable about the tortoise and the hare depicts, going slow may be the winning way. Allowing for snacks, magazines, and a few television shows may just be a good idea.

DROP THE STRUGGLE

Until a few years ago I had spent the greater part of my time in a more or less covert struggle with life. However well things were going, I often felt that something was not quite right. Either I didn't want what turned up in quite the form it appeared, or I wanted something else that never quite materialized in the way I would have hoped. Always there was the pervasive feeling that something was missing, something I couldn't quite put my finger on.

– Roger Housden[25]

In penning the above, poet and author Roger Housden names a reality by which many of us are haunted – the vague sense that something is missing, wrong, or could be better. It's important to acknowledge what we feel. It's healthy to name the emotions that well up within us. Being honest with ourselves when we are displeased is certainly better than pretending all is well. But whether we can put our finger on the cause of our discontent or not, when we choose to focus only on feeling something is missing or not quite right, we fail to appreciate and enjoy the life we have.

To spend time and energy wishing and wanting life to be other than it is, is a recipe for unhappiness. True, there are situations that invite us to put forth effort in order to make them better – a relationship that needs healing, for instance, or an injustice that cannot be tolerated. But the struggle Housden refers to is internal. It is the self-defeating inclination to give power to discontent, to rain on our own parade.

There is no way to prevent feeling disappointed, angry, resentful, and the like, when in fact we are not happy about some aspect of life. However, there is a way to respond to how we feel. We can "drop the struggle." We can let life be life for better or worse. We can accept reality, like it or not. We can love ourselves despite our imperfections. We can let go of our need to control what happens and, instead, go with the flow. We can, in short, learn to *amor fati*, a Latin phrase meaning "love your fate." This is not a matter of resignation, but the radical, courageous willingness to embrace our circumstances painful though they may be. If we drop the struggle, we preserve the energy necessary to make changes.

I had a fantasy recently that I died and was standing at the Pearly Gates where St. Peter said to me, "You know, Tom, it didn't have to be that hard!" There is no escaping the fact that life can be difficult, but by failing to accept what is we sometimes make it harder than it has to be.

ENTER GRACE

In our consumer-driven society, an image of flawless proficiency is crucial to success. To admit failure in a world that judges value by polished surfaces is to lose your edge as a commodity in the marketplace ...

*We're expected to exhibit a quality of perfection we know
we don't possess. All we can do is attempt to hide our sense of
insufficiency. The "imposter syndrome" leaves us juggling
multiple strategies for concealment while warding off a nagging
fear of being "found out." We know we aren't as capable as
people assume (or expect) us to be.*

— Belden Lane[26]

In what he has written, retired theology professor Belden
Lane reveals the inadequacy he felt during his teaching career. Although he managed to be well-thought-of, Lane never
felt at home in the high-powered intellectual atmosphere of
academia. What gave him the courage to confess his hidden
feeling of incompetence was that he knew some version of
the "imposter syndrome" is present in many of us.

The self-consciousness with which we may be burdened
can be experienced not only in our professional life as was
the case with Lane, but also in a personal sense of shame for
misdeeds past or present. In either case, we know we are
often not as "together" as we want to be, or as we might appear to others. The "nagging fear of being found out" can
hang over us like an ominous cloud, whence comes the voice
of judgment and criticism: "You are not as competent, intelligent, or virtuous as you pretend to be!"

What can rescue us from this persistent and self-defeating voice? What, if anything, is powerful enough to coun-
ter its influence? *Enter grace.* Understood as the divinity of
our humanity, the sacredness of our self, grace is an unconditional benevolence from which we cannot and need not
hide. Those aspects of our self we may be ashamed of or
feel self-conscious about can cause us to lose touch with
grace, but nothing can occasion its loss. The sovereignty of
our goodness/Godness is more real than our imperfections.

When it comes to grace, "flawless proficiency" and "polished surfaces" are not the measure of worth. *We don't have to be graceful to be grace-full.* We need only to humbly accept ourselves as flawed in order to be free of being "found out," and in order to become our best selves. For as author Anne Lamott claims, "Grace meets us where we are, but does not leave us where it found us."[27]

EVERY PERSON IS WORTHWHILE

She was sitting at a table, talking with a woman who was, I quickly realized, quite drunk, yet determined to carry on a conversation …

I found myself increasingly confused by what seemed to be an interminable, essentially absurd exchange taking place between the two middle-aged women. When would it end – the alcoholic ranting and the silent nodding … Finally, silence fell upon the room. Dorothy Day asked the woman if she would mind an interruption. She got up and came over to me. She said, "Are you waiting to talk with one of us?"

– Robert Coles[28]

The above is child psychiatrist Robert Coles' account of his first meeting with Dorothy Day, the founder of the Catholic Worker movement. Day was a champion of the poor, the homeless and the unemployed in the Bowery district of Manhattan and beyond, throughout the mid-20th century. Coles was a young medical student when he heard about Day's work. What he encountered when he met her shaped the rest of his life.

In his biography of Day, Coles claims that the words "with one of us" had a profound impact on him and his future work. Though humble and unassuming, Day had a reputation; she was both revered and reviled for her work in the trenches and for her untiring efforts as a peace activist. Dorothy Day was famous. For her to think that Coles may have wanted to speak with the inebriated woman rather than with herself was not a self-effacing statement, but an affirmation of her belief that every person is worthwhile.

As it did for Coles, judgment comes easy for many of us when we encounter people who are drunk, homeless, jobless, or whose appearance or presence is off-putting. We have our personal and societal standards of acceptability, and can find ourselves making unfair assumptions about others from their appearance or behaviour or both. While it is important to acknowledge our reactions and to sometimes be wary of people and situations that could be harmful to us, what is called for more often is understanding, not criticism; compassion, not judgment. As author and inspirational speaker Brad Meltzer states, "Everyone you meet is fighting a battle you know nothing about. Be kind always."

I believe the inclination to judge others is often the result of a failure to embrace our own brokenness, the ways we may not measure up to an ideal. So along with being kind to others it is important to be compassionate toward ourselves – not only on our best days, but on our worst as well.

HOLY FOOLS

Things to Do on an Elevator
1. *Crack open your briefcase or purse, and while peering inside, ask, "Got enough air in there?"*
2. *Meow occasionally.*
3. *Wear a puppet on one of your hands and use it to talk to the other passengers.*

4. *Listen to the elevator walls with a stethoscope.*
5. *Say "ding" at each floor.*
6. *Make noises like an explosion every time someone presses a button.*
7. *Stare, grinning at a friendly passenger, and then announce, "I have on new socks."*
8. *Greet everyone getting on the elevator with a warm handshake and ask each of them to call you "Admiral."*

— Surya Das[29]

My guess is that if you were on an elevator with someone who said or did any of the above, the first thing you would do when you "escaped" would be to alert security! On the other hand, you might find it funny and refreshing to experience a little levity, some lightness in the midst of what is our too often busy and humourless lives.

There is precedent for people who are free-spirited enough to speak and act in a humorous and unconventional manner; they are the archetypical "court jester," the "clown," the "holy fool." It is the purpose of such people not merely to make others laugh, but to cause them to realize that they may be taking themselves and their life too seriously. The jester's message to the king (anyone in a position of authority or power) is that there is a Higher Power they must serve and to which they must answer. The clown demonstrates that life is circus-like and that we need to laugh at our stumbling ways. The holy fool is one whose sometimes heretical words and outrageous actions are a warning that clinging too rigidly to religious beliefs and practices may cause us to become self-righteous and judgmental. Humility, not piety, is the sign of true holiness.

Those whose behaviour challenges us to look closely at the way we live are called iconoclasts. From the Greek *eikon* and *klastes*, the word means "image breaker." When we buy into conventional images of success and acceptability personally, professionally, or religiously, we may need fools to free us from the limiting captivity of convention, for a larger and more fulfilling life.

It's not everyone's calling to be an iconoclast, but if you feel the urge, you might want to *meow* in public places now and then or invite strangers to call you "Admiral." It doesn't have to be April 1st for us to play the fool!

IN DEFENCE OF RUINS

[W]e have lost the enchantment that gives human life meaning and value: We are so intent upon building a well-oiled society – literally and figuratively – that ruins clearly get in the way. They are an obstacle and a nuisance. They represent a regressive movement rather than a forward one, the disabled past rather than the enabling future. Yet maybe our forward progress needs to be disabled, now and then, simply to allow the thoughts and feelings of the deep heart to emerge, providing a grounding of values and the essential element of mystery, without which our progress goes on unhindered and therefore dangerous.

– Thomas Moore[30]

When author and psychotherapist Thomas Moore writes about ruins, he has in mind not only the remnants of old buildings, bridges, stone walls, and other structures, but also the sometimes broken-down state of our personal, professional, spiritual and religious lives. Failed relationships, aging and illness, a career in shambles, a crisis of faith, and other challenging experiences can seem like detours at best from the plans we make for ourselves, "a regressive movement rather than a forward one."

Where we are inclined to see only the negative aspects of decline, Moore senses meaning and importance, for he makes this truly confounding statement: "Maybe our forward progress needs to be disabled, now and then." Ruins don't have to be "an obstacle and a nuisance." Painful though they are, breakups and breakdowns, trials and tribulations, can be the bedrock upon which a new and better self is built, one that is more attentive to relationships, more tolerant of imperfection, and more inclined to enchantment.

When Moore says that without an element of mystery our progress as individuals and as a society is endangered, he is not talking about the unknown, but the sacred. It is often when life individually and collectively is in a state of ruins that we get in touch with the need to reach out, or to reach within to find the source of courage and grace that enables us to confront what must be challenged and to embrace the possibilities to which our dilemmas invite us.

IN PRAISE OF STUMBLING

I get up, I walk, I fall down. Meanwhile I keep dancing.
— Rabbi Hillel
By your stumbling, the world is perfected.
— Sri Aurobindo

British literary legend G. K. Chesterton once wrote, "If a thing is worth doing it is worth doing badly." At first glance this is a confounding statement, for it appears to promote the idea that doing a sloppy job is acceptable. But a closer look reveals the deeper meaning of his words; *doing what is worthwhile is of value even if our doing of it is imperfect.*

Because we breathe the air of a culture that affirms success, applauds perfection, and praises the attainment of ideals, it can be difficult to give ourselves permission to do anything badly. It goes against the grain for most of us to imagine that stumbling can be a dimension of the dance of our life. But achievements are the fruit of effort; they are acquired gradually, and often by trial, error, and failure. In fact, our faulty attempts are what enable us to become more skilled.

This notion extends beyond the realm of tasks to that of ideas. Theoretical physicist Albert Einstein opined that if at first an idea does not sound absurd there is no hope for it. The same concept applies to determination. Author Christopher Morley says, "Big shots are only little shots who keep shooting," and a Japanese proverb states, "Fall down seven times, get up eight."

Hockey great Wayne Gretzky once stated that you miss one hundred percent of the shots you don't take. Striving to do well is important, but when we succumb to the voice of perfectionism, when we allow ourselves to be intimidated by insecurity, and when we give power to the fear of failure, we are less likely to take the shots that help us become better at what we do – and at being who we are.

LAUGHING AT OUR FOLLY

A grandmother playing with her five-year-old grandson on the beach is horrified when a wave comes up and swallows the child whole, dragging him out to sea. Falling to her knees, she addresses the heavens in a state of near hysteria. "Oh God, please return my beloved grandson to me and I will be your devoted supplicant forever and always." Her entreaty heard, the

sky spontaneously clears, a second wave washes up on shore and belches forth the child, returning him unscathed, dry even. The grandmother, elated, faces the horizon once more, and says with the merest trace of impatience, "He had a hat!"
          – David Rakoff[31]

In not being satisfied until the child's hat is returned, the grandmother in this story is a piece of all of us. When we're scared, when we are "in a state of near hysteria," when we are face-to-face with our powerlessness to preserve or pro-tect whom or what we value, we are ready and willing to pledge our all to the All if our pleas for help are answered. But once we are back on familiar and secure ground, it's business as usual – we're in charge again, or so we like to think, and we're not satisfied until we get the hat as well as the child.

This reflection is not an indictment of our fickle na-ture; it is not a reprimand or an encouragement to be more consistently humble even when life is going well. Rather, it is an invitation to laugh at our tendency to forget our vul-nerability and instead to carry on with life in a state of un-conscious denial. Would it be better if we were otherwise, if we walked with a greater sense of reliance on a Higher Power? Perhaps it would be, but that's not who we humans generally are. We tend to schlep along doing our imperfect best to pretend that all is well even when it's not, and to be a tad ungrateful because it's not.

Maybe our inclination to forget our vulnerability and to convince ourselves that we've got it all together is basi-cally healthy. It might just be that being in denial about life's precariousness is better than a constant sense of walking on thin ice. In any case, our "I'll get back to you when things get tough, God, meanwhile where's the hat" attitude is who we are and how we negotiate life on an unstable planet. Better to laugh at our folly than to strive for unattainable perfection. Better to live with a smile than a frown. Better a light heart, than one that is heavy with worry.

LOVING OUR IMPERFECT SELVES

I came here with a huge open heart, like a big, sweet dog, and I still have one. But some days the only thing that can cheer me up is something bad happening to someone I hate, preferably if it went viral and the photo of the person showed hair loss and perhaps the lifelong underuse of sunscreen. My heart still leaps to see this. I often recall the New Yorker cartoon of one dog saying to the other, "It's not enough that we succeed. Cats must also fail."

– Anne Lamott[32]

With her typical wit, honesty, and ability to get to the heart of things, author Anne Lamott gives voice to the shadow, the dark side of our personality, the petty and vindictive self that persists in us despite our desire to be otherwise. We all came here to Mother Earth with a large-hearted innocence, an openness to everything and everyone we encountered. But soon enough, we became less-than-innocent, and more inclined to be not-so-nice.

It's normal to like some people more than others, it's normal to dislike those who in some way offend us, and it's important to keep our distance from those whose presence is toxic to us. But I believe that most of us would like ourselves better if we didn't want our enemies less-than-attractive faces to go viral. Are we stuck with the shadow-self that literary legend C. S. Lewis termed "a zoo of lusts, a bedlam of ambitions, a nursery of fears, a harem of fondled hatreds"?

Is there any hope of overcoming the tendency to take the low road when someone rubs us the wrong way? Maybe yes. Maybe no.

Spiritual disciplines are not a magic bullet. "I meditate, I chant, I drink green tea, and sometimes I still want to smack someone!" Spiritual disciplines can make a difference, of course; they can soften us and make us more responsive and less reactive. But despite our sincere intentions and best efforts, we can sometimes still find ourselves relishing the misfortune of people we dislike.

Nurturing our soul is helpful, but in the end we may just have to learn to love our imperfect selves. It is one of life's wonderful paradoxes that when we love our imperfect selves, what we don't love about ourselves looms less large. When we realize that there is light beneath the shadow, an inner goodness at the same time that we harbour resentments, we become more tolerant and accepting of others. Maybe the cats don't have to fail after all!

MISTAKES AND FORGIVENESS

When I was in medical school, I worked for two months at Yale New Haven Hospital, where I helped take care of an elderly man with chronic pancreatitis. I made the mistake of assigning him a regular diet, not the very-low-fat diet his condition required. When he was served pork chops, he ate them with gusto, and abdominal pain followed. I felt terrible. As I rewrote his orders, I was almost in tears. The attending physician laughed at my distress, saying, "I hope this is the worst mistake you make as a doctor!" (It wasn't.)

Later I entered the patient's room to apologize to him and his concerned daughter.

"Are you kidding?" his daughter asked. "He knew he

wasn't supposed to eat a pork chop! Don't worry about it!"
Mistakes are our teachers; forgiveness helps us learn.
– Karen Miller[33]

Though upsetting at the time, physician Karen Miller's experience as a medical student led her to the kind of wisdom that applies to every aspect of life. Whether in our personal or professional lives, we all make mistakes. Mistakes are a given. Mistakes are what we flirt with when we decide to get out of bed in the morning. Making mistakes are what often happens when we attempt to do our best.

Unlike mistakes, forgiveness is not a given – it is an option. We can choose to humbly acknowledge our failings and thus be free to learn from them, or we can fan the flame of blame, in which case we become focused on ourselves in judgmental and critical ways. We can spend a lifetime in negative self-talk, running in circles of "woulda, coulda, shoulda."

What Miller came to realize was that mistakes can be a *felix culpa*, a happy fault, if we forgive ourselves for making them. Mistakes can be a source of wisdom, the means by which we discover a better way to do what we do. Forgiveness enables us to move forward with insight, humility, and compassion.

ODE TO JOY

The anonymous author of the following quote turns the traditional image of spirituality on its head: "God and the angels will hold you accountable for all the joys you were allowed in life that you denied yourself."

Instead of the solemn face of the saint or the figure of a renunciate lost in contemplation, he gives us the image of joy as

the gateway to heaven. The experience of joy in this world is an indication that our spirit is shining brightly. Joy is an expression of our deepest nature, beyond all notions of right and wrong, beyond all dogma and belief, beyond any religious framework … Joy is a pure expression of the human spirit.
— Roger Housden[34]

Allowing ourselves to experience joy is no easy task when a pandemic, racial inequities and injustice, global warming, terrorism, and other weighty issues are so viscerally on our minds and hearts. There is so much to be sad and mad about that joy seems like the last thing that can or should be front and centre. But if poet Roger Housden and the anonymous author he quotes are correct, "joy is an expression of our deepest nature" and is therefore too important to lose touch with, too close to the bone of who we are as human-spiritual beings.

It is not only spirituality that gets turned upside down when joy is considered something to embrace, for the conventional wisdom of our time and culture clearly prioritizes the likes of seriousness, logic, responsibility, and hard work. Joy may be the "gateway to heaven," but a frown not a smile is the sign that we are earnest citizens of the earth.

True joy is not the opposite of accountability, dependability, and other elements of maturity; it is not a Pollyanna-like outlook, but a radical quality of character, an unquenchable vitality, enthusiasm, and passion for life that the French refer to as *joie de vivre*. Joy is more a matter of choice than of feeling; we can choose to be joyful even amidst life's difficulties and demands.

Joy is what we can experience when we are connected to the sacred depth that poet Robert Frost refers to when he says, "We dance 'round in a ring and suppose. But the secret sits in the middle and knows."[35] The "secret" at the heart of who we are, which is present even when we don't feel it, is that divinity is the D in our DNA. God, by whatever name, is our essence. If instead of keeping this "secret" a secret we gave ourselves permission to live it, joy might just help us remain positive and hopeful in the midst of life's very real and often dire circumstances.

PURE PRAYER

A priest of the Greek Orthodox Church ... tells of a monk he met on Mount Athos. He was in a very bad state, very dark, very bitter, very angry. When asked what was the matter, he said, "Look at me; I've been here for thirty-eight years, and I have not yet attained pure prayer." And this other fellow on the pilgrimage was saying how sad he thought this was. Another man present said, "It's a sad story all right, but the sadness consists in the fact that after thirty-eight years in a monastery he's still interested in pure prayer."

– Ernest Kurtz and Katherine Ketcham[36]

Interest in pure prayer, or pure anything for that matter, strikes me as worthy of aspiration. Whether in the realm of our personal, professional, or religious and spiritual lives, what could be better than striving for perfection, attempting to excel, reaching for an ideal? But according to this Hasidic story such efforts may be problematic. What is sad about this monk is not that he failed to "attain pure prayer," but that after such a long time in a place dedicated to drawing close to God, he still did not realize that our failures, our brokenness, our being less-than-perfect are a doorway to the divine.

This lesson is one that another monk in a different monastery learned and communicated to me when I asked him whether, after the 30 years he had spent in monastic life, he felt God's presence more than when he first took his vows. I was surprised when he responded "no," and I was dumbfounded when he went on to say, "but now it doesn't matter." His saying "it doesn't matter" did not mean that he didn't care, but that he had come to realize that what is important is not attaining the ideal of a felt sense of closeness to God, but living with the conviction that we are never without God, whether we feel it or not.

"There's nowhere to go, nothing to attain, no one to become" is a Buddhist saying that affirms the wisdom of not striving. Because the spiritual fullness we seek is a reality where we are, as we are, and as who we are, and because God is a word for an ever-present spiritual reality, we need but look beneath the surface of our imperfect selves to see and to sense that despite our not attaining "pure prayer," we're just fine.

SINCERELY YOURS

My only regret in life is that I'm not someone else.
– Woody Allen

Although the art of letter writing is something of a casualty in this age of emails, at some point in our life we are likely to have signed off at the end of a missive with the word "sincerely," which indicates that we mean what we have stated, that it is truthful and heartfelt. But the derivation of the word sincere refers not to veracity or to feeling, but to our imperfect self. To be sincere is to be without guile or pretense. Sincerity refers to our willingness to be our less-than-ideal self – what you see is what you get.

Happiness, satisfaction, inner peace and the like do not

depend on looking good or being perfect, but on acceptance of our imperfection. These things are the fruit of honestly acknowledging – to ourselves first of all, and to others when appropriate – not only our strengths, but our weaknesses as well. We need not broadcast our imperfection to the world, but it can be a relief to do so with a trusted other. It feels good to be admired, but it is better to be known.

Accepting character faults such as having a temper, being petty, insecure, fearful, impatient, and the like, is no small task. The message most of us have internalized from family, religion, and society in general is that faults like these, if they cannot be corrected, should be hidden from view. But when we refuse to fully embrace ourselves, when we live with a sense of shame because we do not measure up to some ideal, we tend to become self-critical, self-deprecating, and self-absorbed. That's way too much self! In this case we might find ourselves resonating with filmmaker and comedian Woody Allen's statement, "My only regret in life is that I'm not someone else!"

Changing for the good is good, but growth begins with the embrace of ourselves as we are. Before we can be honest with another, "sincerely yours," we must be "sincerely mine," that is, honest with our self.

STUMBLING BLOCKS OR BUILDING BLOCKS

The Red Sea only parts when you're in water over your head.
– source unknown

You may have heard the saying that the difference between stumbling blocks and building blocks is the way we use them. What I view as insurmountable may be so only because I allow it to be. I don't know one alcoholic who prefers to have a drinking problem, but I know many who have embraced the fact of their alcoholism and are now helping others who struggle with that addiction. Likewise, I don't know anyone who is content to have cancer, but I know a number of cancer survivors who now live every day of their lives gratefully, and who counsel others to do the same. These are but two of the many ways we can turn personal tragedies into triumphs, two examples of how stumbling blocks can become building blocks that make of our life an enduring edifice.

Our initial instinct is, of course, to react against what is hurtful, unfair, and unexpected – no one wants what is difficult. But, with the passage of time, we can become better able to see with different eyes, to recognize opportunity and possibility, to glimpse light where there was once only darkness. Choosing to embrace life's difficulties, however, does not guarantee that the going will be smooth. Using imagery from the Old Testament, some sage once said, "the Red Sea only parts when you're in water over your head." The way forward may be murky but putting one foot in front of the other leads to freedom.

The examples mentioned above – addiction and illness – serve to highlight what can happen when we respond to life's difficulties as a doorway to a new and positive path. But what is true personally is also true collectively. Think pandemic. We can bemoan the limiting reality of this event and we can huddle in fear against its pervasive danger, or we can, along with being careful, be open to the lessons it may offer about our vulnerability (we are at the same time resilient and fragile), our common bond with all humanity (the same things cause us pain and bring us joy no matter what country we call home), and the importance of reaching out to those most in need (we may not be able to "fix" them, but we can all do something for someone).

THE CROOKED PATH HOME

In the chapters to come, I speak often of my own mistakes – of wrong turns I have taken, of misreading my own reality – for hidden in these moments are important clues to my own vocation. I do not feel despondent about my mistakes ... though I grieve the pain they have sometimes caused others. Our lives are "experiments with truth" (to borrow the subtitle of Gandhi's autobiography), and in an experiment negative results are at least as important as successes. I have no idea how I would have learned the truth about myself and my calling without the mistakes I have made ...

– Parker Palmer[37]

Writer, teacher, and activist Parker Palmer begins his book *Let Your Life Speak* by acknowledging that the path that led him to clarity about himself was not without detours. My guess is that most of us would rather reach our goals without going off track. Success not failure, clarity not confusion, winning not losing, right turns not wrong ones, are our preferred course of travel. What could make more sense than wanting to get where we're going without becoming lost?

Palmer's "experiments with truth" have taught him that only when we fail to achieve our goals are we poised to learn what are arguably life's most important lessons – humility and compassion. Humility, the down-to-earth acceptance of our strengths and weakness, and compassion, the loving embrace of our own and others' less than ideal selves, are our *raison d'etre*, the reason for our being. When we measure the success of our lives by any other standard, we miss the most profound purpose of our existence.

The saying "God's ways are not our ways" speaks to the importance of "the crooked path." This does not mean there is Someone in the heavens pulling strings that result in our failure or confusion in order to bring us to our knees. Rather, it names the truth that the only way to become our God-self, the sacred person we are meant to be, is by meeting face-to-face the limits of our willpower, efforts, and best intentions. These inner resources are important for achieving our goals. However, it is not what we accomplish, but what we overcome that matters most.

If we accept its teaching, failure in its many forms – relational, professional, spiritual – can be the portal to our soul, the doorway through which we must pass if we are to discover and become our sacred selves.

THE MASTER LIMPS

Who is the spiritual master? The master limps. The master is not perfect. Like the rest of us, the master is flawed. But unlike most of us, the master is not handicapped by his limping because he knows his limping doesn't have the power to name who he is. Like everyone else, the master is confused. But unlike us, the master is not confused by her confusion because she knows her confusion doesn't have the power to name who she is. As is the case with the rest of humanity, the master is afraid of many things, but the master is not frightened by his fear because he knows his fear doesn't have the power to name who he is.
– James Finley[38]

The words above are paraphrased from a talk given by psychologist James Finley. Jim, a long-time friend, is making a case for the fact that a person need not be without normal feelings to be a spiritual master or guide – that is, one who is anchored in a sense of self that is sacred. Being "handicapped" is a metaphor for what happens when we identify with what inhibits us, thereby limiting our understanding of who we are. We do not have to have overcome our humanness to be spiritually attuned; neither do we have to be without a limp (flaw) to be a person who can help others get in touch with their spiritual depth.

The difference between those who can face life's perplexities without being thrown by them and the rest of us is that they know they are more than their confusion, fear, insecurity, inadequacy, self-doubt, and the like. Those who are spiritually attuned know that, like an iceberg, beneath their own surface lies a dimension of their being that is solid and sacred. No one is immune from the feelings that come with being human, but all of us are more than those feelings. When we lose touch with this truth, our sense of self becomes trapped at the surface, and we become handicapped by our limping.

All of this begs the question how we can keep from giving power to the tendency to identify with limiting feelings and self-concepts? There is no easy answer to this query, but there is a way to respond to it. First, we must accept our feelings. Second, we must resist the impulse to identify with them. Acceptance means acknowledging our fear, confusion, and any other difficult emotions that may arise. Paradoxically, we do not lessen the impact of such feelings by overcoming them. Rather, we do so by facing them. Resisting means refusing to buy into the notion that we are what we feel, and affirming over, and over, and over again, that there is more to us than our limp.

TO ERR IS HUMAN

Imagine a different world, one in which people do not spend an inordinate amount of energy fuming against their fate each time they make a mistake. A world in which one takes for granted that if things can go wrong, they probably will.

It would be so civilized. Folks would bump into furniture, miss deadlines, get lost on the way to the airport, forget to return phone calls, and show up at parties a day early, without getting unduly annoyed with themselves.

Dream on. This forgiving world is as utopian as Shangri-La. Though we all agree that to err is human, each of us individually believes that he or she is the exception ... Make a mistake? Not on my watch!

– Veronique Vienne[39]

Why is it so hard to cut ourselves some slack? Why are most of us prone to think and feel that if we bump into furniture, miss deadlines, or get lost that not only are these things not okay, but *we're* not okay? It's true that when such things happen we are probably not at the top of our game, but show me the person who is always at the top of their game and I'll show you someone who is painfully intense and likely very judgmental.

In her book *The Art of Imperfection*, author Veronique Vienne sings the praises of relaxation, chilling out, lightening-up, being more Zen. All of which is easier said than done. "Wired" is a word that comes to mind when I ponder our propensity for perfection. "Driven" is another. When we are unable or unwilling to allow ourselves room to fall short of being our ideal self, we flirt with stress and burnout, if we're lucky – a stroke or heart attack if we're not.

It's not a question of whether or not we will stumble,

but of when and how often. Given the inevitability of our faltering ways, it becomes essential for the health of body, mind, and soul that we develop the capacity for self-compassion, the willingness to forgive ourselves, and the ability to laugh at our folly.

The saying "to err is human" is not an acknowledgement that humanity is flawed, nor is it permission to be a slacker. Rather, it is an invitation to cut ourselves some slack, and to revel in the truth that the human condition, though less-than-ideal, is pretty amazing nonetheless.

TORN TO PIECES

The spirituality of imperfection speaks to those who seek meaning in the absurd, peace within the chaos, light within the darkness, joy within the suffering … This is not a spirituality for saints or gods, but for people who suffer from what the philosopher-psychologist William James called "torn-to-pieces-hood" … We have all known that experience, for to be human is to feel at times divided, fractured, pulled in a dozen directions … and to yearn for serenity, for some healing.
— Ernest Kurtz and Katherine Ketcham[40]

"Torn-to-pieces-hood" is a "hood" I'd rather not live in. Being divided, fractured, and pulled in a dozen directions is not my idea of a good time, but like them or not, trials such as these come with the territory of the imperfect world we inhabit. There's no way around it; from time to time, life can be overwhelming.

Spirituality is often considered a way to escape our woes, a comfortable cocoon, a realm of refuge where we can experience serenity and healing. Spirituality thus understood is a feel-good venture that can dispel, at least for a time, the absurdity, chaos, darkness, and suffering that authors Ernest Kurtz and Katherine Ketcham refer to. Nothing wrong with a little serenity, but true, healthy, mature spirituality is not an escape from life; it is not about rising above our pain, but entering into it to such a degree that we experience the meaning, peace, light, and joy that lie beneath the surface of what and how we feel, when what and how we feel doesn't feel so good.

Unlike the brand of spirituality that tries to make everything feel better, the spirituality of imperfection is imperfect, meaning it is not a "fix," it is not a palliative, it does not pretend to heal what hurts. Instead, it affirms that in the midst of life's trials and tragedies there is a sacredness that can sustain us. To experience this sustaining presence, we have to be still, quiet, and open. No easy task when we feel "torn-to-pieces."

THREE

AWAKE TO THE MYSTERY IN OUR MIDST

PSYCHOLOGIST AND SPIR-
ITUAL TEACHER JAMES FINLEY HAS WHIMSICALLY SAID,
"BE WHERE YOU IS, 'CUZ IF YOU AIN'T WHERE YOU IS, YOU
IS WHERE YOU AIN'T." Mindfulness is the popular term for
the discipline of recollection, of being fully present to where
we are, who we're with, and what we're doing. Because "God"
is a word for the spiritual essence of all creation, it is when
we are wholeheartedly present to life that we are poised to
experience the divine depth that underlies every aspect of it.

Because we most often "ain't where we is," we can easily
come to the end of our day, and days, feeling that we have
missed something essential, something sacred, something
that was hidden in plain sight. It is no easy task to practice
the asceticism of place and time – "be here now" – but this
manner of living can bring new life to life.

The reflections that follow are meant as a reminder to
return our wandering minds and hearts to the present moment, for in doing so we might encounter the stunning truth
that heaven is here.

A CONTEMPLATIVE WAY OF LIFE

*Learning to live a more contemplative way of life in the midst of
today's world – what could be more simple or more difficult?
Simple because the contemplative way is the way of seeing what
simply is ... It is the way of being who we simply are in the
rhythmic simplicity of our breathing, in the sovereign simplicity
in which day gives way to night and night to day.*

Simple, too, is the manner of entering into this ever-present Way. It consists of learning to sit and be, to slow down and settle into the precious givenness of who we are right now, just the way we are. It consists of … letting go of the tangled web of noise and concerns that seemingly hold us in its grasp.
— James Finley[41]

Psychologist and former monk James Finley describes the simple but difficult task of living "a contemplative way of life." Until I became more acquainted with the term "contemplative," I thought it referred only to the lifestyle of monks and cloistered nuns. It was, in my mind, a stark existence consisting of chanting psalms, doing demanding manual labour, maintaining silence, and spending long hours in private prayer, the sum of which struck me as anything but simple.

I have now come to realize, as Finley indicates, that being contemplative is not primarily about a "monkish" lifestyle but about living with an awareness that there is a sacredness to the simple rhythm of our breathing, in the quiet way in which night and day give way to one another, and in our being the person we are, flaws and all. Divinity is present in the natural flow of life.

What keeps us from sensing this sacred presence? What makes it so difficult to experience the nearness of the holiness with which everything and everyone is imbued? I believe our inability to connect with the sacred in our midst has to do in part with the fact that many of us learned that spirit and matter are separate from one another, and that the former is separate from rather than part of our earthy existence. I also believe that the "tangled web of noise and concerns" that comes with the territory of our hectic lives makes it next to impossible to sense the sacredness of who we are and where we are.

It is by living a simple life – "learning to sit and be, to slow down" – that we are most likely to sense the sacred. It is when we are mindfully present to the present moment of our lives that the divine depth that underlies all creation may emerge from hiding long enough to bless us with a glimpse of itself.

BE HERE NOW

Having almost died from cancer, having landed back in life, having been humbled to accept my fragility as a simple being in an infinite world of simple beings, I confess that I'm investigating the risks of being here simply because my experience has led me to believe that entering this life fully and deeply is the surest way to feel the presence of all that is eternal ...

As I tried to inquire into what it means to be here, our dog would tug at me like a wordless sage, demanding that I stop writing and just be! ... Almost daily, she would knock the pen from my hand ... coaxing me to get on the floor and hold her and stare into her animal eyes, which would say everything and nothing in the most innocent of ways.

– Mark Nepo[42]

When poet and author Mark Nepo had a brush with death, he became aware that nothing is more important than being here now. Being an intelligent and articulate man, Nepo began to ponder this realization, to consider its ramifications, and to find ways to put his insights into words. He wondered how he could have failed to realize this basic truth for so long and how he might hold on to it so as to "feel the presence of all that is eternal"?

In the midst of his speculation, enter his dog, Mira, which in Spanish means "look." Nepo was intellectualizing something that needed to be experienced. He was thinking and writing about living life fully and deeply but wasn't doing so! Mira invited him to look at life, to get out of his head and onto the floor where he could live what he was pondering and where he might discover the earthy wisdom of poet William Blake who wrote, "Eternity is in love with the productions of time."

The floor is a metaphor for the ground upon which we walk at home and at work, both inside and outdoors. The floor is where our relationships unfold, where we carry out our responsibilities, where we encounter life's trials, tragedies, and triumphs. The floor is under our feet and before our eyes; it is the place where, if our hearts are open, we may encounter the spirituality of reality.

I suppose it could be said that Mira, as real as she is, is also a metaphor. Mira is every person, or pet for that matter, who calls us to respond to their needs. When we are preoccupied with our own thoughts, when perhaps without knowing it we're living in our head rather than our bodies, Mira can feel like an interruption rather than an invitation. But anyone or anything that beckons us to be present to them is the voice of God calling us to get on the floor, to look at life with "animal eyes," and to be here now.

BEING WHOLLY ALIVE

The most solid advice for a writer is this, I think: Try to learn to breathe deeply, really to taste food when you eat, and when you sleep really to sleep. Try as much as possible to be wholly alive with all your might, and when you laugh, laugh like hell. And when you get angry, get good and angry. Try to be alive. You will be dead soon enough.

– William Saroyan[43]

When he encourages us to "try as much as possible to be wholly alive," Pulitzer Prize-winning author and playwright William Saroyan offers good advice not only for writers but for all of us. It seems so simple, so obvious, such a no-brainer to experience what we're doing and how we're feeling. Why would we need encouragement, why would we need to be reminded to live?

The obvious answer to this question is that we need reminders because we forget. We need wake-up calls because we fall asleep to the wonder at the heart of life's most basic functions, which in health care are known as ADLs (activities of daily living). When asked by a disciple about the method of Buddhism, the teacher responded, "We stand, we sit, we bathe, we walk." The student then stated, "I do those things, too." Said the teacher in reply, "When we stand, we know we are standing ... " This depth of awareness can turn our activities of daily living into spiritual practices, for knowing is not merely a matter of the mind but of experiencing a sensual sensitivity to the incarnate sacredness of life.

The method of Buddhism is also the heart of Christianity, Judaism, Islam, and all the world's great religions. There is often an otherworldly focus to traditional religious teachings, an emphasis on the afterlife and on what we must do to earn a soft landing there. But the mystical dimension of all traditions shifts the focus of the spiritual life to the here and now, and to the importance of being as present as possible to the mundane activities required to maneuver through the day.

We may not think of them in this way, but breathing, tasting our food, sleeping, laughing like hell, and getting good and angry, are all aspects of life that are as holy as they are human. For while we are alive, it is here not there, it is now not later, it is in our bodies not out of them that we have the once-in-a-lifetime opportunity to be spiritually, wholly alive.

BETWEEN BIRTH AND DEATH

[E]cology merges with spirituality, because the experience of being connected with all of nature, of belonging to the universe, is the very essence of spirituality. The original meaning of spirit in many ancient philosophical and religious traditions, in the West as well as in the East, is that of the breath of life. The Latin word **spiritus,** *the Greek word* **psyche,** *and the Sanskrit* **atman** *all mean breath. Our spiritual moments are those moments when we feel most intensely alive.*

– Fritjof Capra[44]

What is it that comedian George Carlin said? "Life is measured not by the number of breaths we take, but by the number of moments that take our breath away." There aren't many moments in life that take our breath away. Few experiences stop us in our tracks, make us do a doubletake, bring us to our knees. Birth and death are two that come to mind, for as naturally and frequently as they usually occur, there is a dramatic element to both, and when they happen to us, they are once-in-a-lifetime events.

But what about those less-than-dramatic occurrences that populate so much of our day? What about the *many-in-a-lifetime* happenings? Are they not amazing in their own subtle way, and do we not miss out on being "intensely alive" when we fail to notice them? So many things happen between the bookends of birth and death that could, if we were attentive to them, make us realize that we are "connected with all of nature."

It is our partial presence to the events that take place and to the people we meet every day that keeps us from sensing that we are a part of something larger than ourselves. When we are only "sort of" where we are, we cannot experience the wonder of being where we are. When we are only "kind of" with whomever we are with, we miss out on the uniqueness of that person. And when we are "crazy busy," we fail to experience the *spiritus, psyche, atman* – the spiritual depth of every breath and of everything we do.

It is often thought that being spiritual means rising above the realm of the ordinary and the earthy. But if physicist Fritjof Capra is right about connection and belonging being the essence of spirituality, then the ability to engage not separate, to bond with life and relationships not to detach from them, are signs that we are evolving spiritually. This truth is central to all wisdom traditions and is expressed in a down-to-earth way in the saying, "Zen does not confuse spirituality with thinking about God while you're peeling potatoes. Spirituality is peeling potatoes!"

CONTEMPLATIVE BY CATASTROPHE

I'm a "contemplative by catastrophe." My wake-up calls generally come after the wreck has happened and I'm trying to dig my way out of the debris. I do not recommend this path as a conscious choice. But if you, dear reader, have a story similar to mine, I come as the bearer of glad tidings. Catastrophe, too, can be a contemplative path, pitched and perilous as it may be.

Life can always be counted on to send something my way – who knows what it will be today? Maybe a reminder of a part of my past that I regret. Maybe a spot-on critique of something I thought I did well. Maybe a political outrage that makes me feel that my country has lost all semblance of soul.

> *Whatever it is I'll try to work my way through it until a*
> *hopeful reality is revealed on the other side. Regret can be*
> *turned into blessing. Criticism can refocus our work or*
> *strengthen our resolve. When we feel certain that the human*
> *soul is no longer at work in the world, it's time to make sure*
> *that ours is visible to someone, somewhere.*
>
> – Parker Palmer[45]

There are many meanings for the word "contemplation." In common parlance it refers to an intense focus, an attempt to decipher the depth of a subject. Religiously, contemplation is a form of meditative prayer characterized by quiet, wordless stillness wherein one rests in the presence of God. From a spiritual perspective, which is the one taken by Quaker author Parker Palmer, contemplation is the experience of awakening to the truth that both our life and life itself have a sacred depth of which we are most often unaware.

It is sometimes thought that the wake-up call to this depth comes in the form of a gentle nudge when, for instance, we are smitten by the beauty of a sunset, surprised by an act of kindness, or stopped in our tracks by the birth of a child or the peaceful, timely death of an aged loved one. Events of this sort, ordinary yet miraculous, can pull the rug from under our everyday, sleepwalking way of getting through life.

This is not Palmer's experience, as he states that "catastrophe, too, can be a contemplative path." It can be the painfully unexpected, unwanted, and unfair that opens our eyes, minds, and hearts to the wonder of it all. Even the likes of regret, criticism, and outrage can be a blessing that makes us aware and appreciative of the sacredness of life, of others, and of ourselves. What is important is not how these wake-up calls come but that we recognize and respond to them as invitations to become more present to the mystery of ordinary life.

EVERYTHING HAS A SONG

A plant scientist, armed with his notebooks and equipment, is exploring the rainforests for new botanical discoveries, and he has hired an Indigenous guide to lead him. Knowing the scientist's interests, the young guide takes care to point out the interesting species. The botanist looks at him appraisingly, surprised by his capacity. "Well, well, young man, you certainly know the names of a lot of these plants." The guide nods and replies with downcast eyes. "Yes, I have learned the names of all the bushes, but I have yet to learn their songs."
— Robin Wall Kimmerer[46]

What might it mean to say that bushes have songs as author and botanist Robin Wall Kimmerer posits in this story? And what about trees, plants, and animals, and what about human beings? Do we all have songs too?

"Song" in this instance is a metaphor, a figure of speech referring to the animating source of life that radiates from deep within all living things. Such songs are synonymous with soul, and what our soul songs "sing," though not audible, is nonetheless detectable if we listen with what St. Benedict called the "ear of the heart." All creation resonates with the sacred essence of life. If we listen deeply, we may perceive creation's song despite the incessant noise within and around us.

From the Latin *per sonare*, the word "person" means to "sound through." Life's song does not come *from* us but *through* us. Annie Dillard refers to this truth when she writes, "Something pummels us, something barely sheathed. Power broods and lights. We are played on like a pipe; our breath is not our own."[47]

We are breathed into, we are enlivened with the life of the Spirit, we are instruments through which a sacred, silent sound is emitted.

The guide in the story above is said to have "downcast eyes" because he has not learned the songs of the bushes. It is sad when we fail to sense creation's sacredness, for if we are not attuned to it we miss the celestial truth that its collective sound is not that of a chorus but of a choir, and that it gives voice not so much to a song but to a hymn announcing the presence of the Holy.

IF YOU HANKER

If you hanker for
a zenith of felicity
on the bed of the Divine
begin by dusting off
the wings of wonder
on your local pillow
Lift your ineffable
out of the mundane
Aim for airborne
with the eye of the heart
as your sky pilot
and soar to glory.

– James Broughton[48]

Poet James Broughton uses lofty language to convey a very down-to-earth message: if we want to experience the height of joy that is oneness with the divine, don't overlook life in the here and now. In the midst of the mundane, in the places where we live and work, in the people we encounter every day, here on our "local pillow" lies the ineffable mystery for which "God" is a word.

We may have to do some dusting off to discover the glory of which Broughton writes. We may have to look through different eyes than the ones we've used all our life. We may have to rethink our understanding of creation in order to glimpse the great truth – that for which we hanker is here. Heaven, Henry David Thoreau has said, is under our feet as well as over our head.

It takes some doing to see and appreciate the divinity of our life in the world. It is nothing less than radical to affirm wonder beneath the injustice and cruelty, the tragedy and travesty that too often characterize our existence. But without denying life's harsh realities, is it not amazing that seeds of new life often follow in the footsteps of death, that compassion rises up to meet suffering, and that despair, in time, can give way to hope?

Experiencing "a zenith of felicity on the bed of the Divine" need not wait until the world is perfect, or until we are no longer a part of it, for there is wonder aplenty on our "local pillow." If we look "with the eye of the heart" we can "soar to glory" even while our feet are on the ground.

LEARNING LIFE'S LESSONS

I've learned to better compartmentalize which ... means focusing on the things I can control and ignoring what I can't ... I've learned how important it is to sit and eat with other people ... I've learned that most problems aren't rocket science ... I've learned that grass smells great and wind feels amazing and rain is a miracle ... I've learned a new empathy for other people, including people I don't know, people I don't like, and people I disagree with.

– Scott Kelly[49]

Astronaut Scott Kelly learned the life lessons he mentions in the quotation above, and many more besides, while circling the earth for a record 340 days. Time and distance from normal existence were his teachers, outer space was his school, and NASA's International Space Station was his classroom. The lessons Kelly learned aren't extraordinary or, pardon the pun, "out of this world," for the art of compartmentalization, the joy of sharing a meal, the sensual appreciation of nature, and empathy for others are the stuff of life here on earth.

British politician Andrew Bennett once claimed that "the longest journey you will ever take is the 18 inches from your head to your heart." It took the perspective his extended journey afforded for Kelly's lessons to travel that short but immense distance. Intellectual knowledge is one thing, but true knowing affects who we are and how we choose to live. This is what took place for Kelly.

It's not likely that any of us will have the opportunity to experience outer space, but that doesn't mean we can't learn to appreciate the people, places, and things we encounter every day. We don't have to be absent from our routines and relationships to realize their significance, but we may have to retreat into the "inner space" of our minds and hearts to recall and re-member (connect again) the importance of those people and things to which we have grown accustomed.

LONGING FOR WHOLENESS

*Everyone wants to feel the fullness of a life fully lived. The
difference is in the strategy. Most think that fame and fortune
will be their flowering. Others see their fruit to be in their
family. Some strike out on wild adventures, while a few devote
themselves to prayer and meditation. Whatever the method, the
aim is fundamentally the same – to satisfy a longing for
wholeness. We can chase many rainbows before we realize that
what we truly want, however, lies in the one place we never
thought to look. The flower of our life is already in bud even
now, precisely in our present circumstances.*

– Roger Housden[50]

The above quote from poet Roger Housden reminds me
of the saying, "What we reach for may be different, but what
makes us reach is the same." What we think will make us
happy varies from person to person depending in large part
on the messages we have received and the values we have
learned from family, peers, faith communities, and society
in general; but the inner hunger that fuels our reaching, the
longing for wholeness, the craving for gratification, the
homesickness for what is ultimate – that inner hunger is
universal.

To claim that there is a common inner desire for wholeness is to say that there is an incompleteness that comes
with the territory of being human. Housden claims that no
matter what the differences between us (gender, race, religion, sexual orientation, etc.), there lurks within an
unsettledness that drives us to seek fullness through fame
and fortune, building our families, striking out on wild adventures, or devoting ourselves to a life of prayer. Something
seems to be missing. We chase after many "rainbows" in an

attempt to satisfy our longing for wholeness and in the process we often overlook what is right in front of us.

Hidden in plain sight, disguised in the apparel of the ordinary, cloaked in the dress of everyday life, is that for which we yearn. This is a perplexing claim, since the wholeness for which we long is usually thought to be beyond us rather than within, far off not close at hand. This misconception often sends us on an addictive search for what we think or feel is missing, instead of looking more intently at what we have and who we are. What is missing, in other words, is not something we don't have but sensitivity to the spiritual fullness that is the ground of our "present circumstances."

It may not feel like it in the midst of hard times, but if it's true that "the flower of our life is already in bud even now," we would do well to stop and smell the roses.

LOOK FOR THE GOOD

Puritanism is the haunting fear that someone,
somewhere, may be happy!
– H. L. Mencken[51]

The spiritual life, it is thought, is another kind of life than the one we experience with its cares and concerns, its responsibilities and relationships, its demands and delights But when spirituality is divorced from the everyday dimension of our lives, we are like a plant uprooted from the soil. When cut off from the source of life we tend to become lifeless, joyless, and critical. Journalist H. L. Mencken took aim at this phenomenon when he said, "Puritanism is the haunting fear that someone, somewhere, may be happy!" We do not give testimony to the Spirit when our spirits are glum.

The enjoyment of what this world offers and the recognition of its goodness is an affirmation that God is its Essence. The denial of life's goodness is a denial of its Godness.

Here in the Western world, a significant dose of Puritanism seems to have crept into the minds and hearts of those who sincerely strive to live the ideals of their religious tradition. Everything from drinking to dancing to playing cards, not to mention sensuality and sexuality, is sometimes thought to be tainted. That we, or someone somewhere, are happy should make us happy, but the enjoyment of life's pleasures is not high on a Puritanical list of things considered sacred.

As we move through life, we encounter many challenges, many difficulties, many heartbreaking situations that require us to dig deep if we are to meet them with some semblance of grace. If we're not careful we can begin to lose sight of the goodness and "Godness" of life. When that happens, we live, instead, in fear of the next hurtful occurrence and miss the opportunity to savour life's many delights.

A friend sent me an email recently reminding me to look for the good, the wonder, and the beauty hidden in plain sight – the little things that may not be so small after all. His message read, "Hug your pillow. Enjoy the morning cappuccino. Listen carefully when the wind blows. Kiss a tree. Love the one you're with – life is getting shorter every day."

Theologian Paul Tillich coined the phrase "Ground of Being" as a way of conceiving of God not as a person far off in the heavens but as the essence of everything and everyone. "God" is a word for the sacred ground, the soil, the spiritual substance at the heart of all creation. This notion of the divine invites us to enjoy life, not merely to endure it. It summons us to revel in life's pleasures as well as to be present for the tough stuff. It calls us to sense, with our senses, the supernatural nature of nature – human and otherwise. We touch God when we are in touch with life.

Yes, our lives are getting shorter every day, but in every one of those days we can stumble upon the divinity of the ordinary by engaging, enjoying, relishing, and basking in life's "cares and concerns, its responsibilities and relationships, its demands and delights."

MORE FLESHY THAN FLASHY

Two good signs that we don't truly believe God is already present to us are our popular assumptions (1) that any genuine experience of God must be a flashy, road-to-Damascus encounter, and (2) that this lightning-bolt kind of epiphany is possible only by submitting to the spiritual equivalent of a boot camp obstacle course. Nothing less than skyrocketing ascents to beatific visions satisfies our sense of propriety, and we just assume that the only way to get off the launch pad is to subdue earthbound flesh with harshly ascetic or elaborately choreographed spiritual techniques …

Our demand for pyrotechnics is based on the erroneous assumption that humans are so radically separated from God … that the gulf can be bridged only by intense spiritual explosions that catapult us out of the everyday straight toward the divine core.

– Kerry Walters[52]

Philosophy professor Kerry Walters penned these words for his book about 20th-century Quaker mystic Rufus Jones. As is evident from this quote, Jones was a down-to-earth mystic, not one whose sense of God and religion was esoteric or other worldly. Jones would say we discover divinity *here* not *there*, *now* not *later*, at home and at work not just in places of worship – in the fleshy not the flashy.

Dramatic religious or spiritual experiences do happen as was the case for Paul on the road to Damascus (Acts 9:3-9). But such encounters, if they happen at all, are few and far between, and in conventional religious thinking are considered a reward for our efforts. In this scheme, the more we pray, the more we sacrifice, the harder we try, the more likely we are to get a peek at the hidden God. It is a game of hide-and-seek, and whether or not we find God depends on our determination and persistence.

What is important is not the occurrence of spiritual "close encounters" but that we recognize the more frequent and subtle disclosures of the divinity of ordinary life. Because seeing the same people, doing the same tasks, travelling the same route day in and day out tends to desensitize us to the spiritual landscape of life, it is no small accomplishment to sense the sacredness of someone or something to which we've grown accustomed.

Artist Georgia O'Keeffe knew there is no gulf to be bridged between heaven and earth, and that experiencing the sacredness of something as common as a flower or a friend is not a matter of "harshly ascetic or elaborately choreographed spiritual techniques." O'Keeffe knew the value of simply slowing down and gazing deeply: "Nobody sees a flower – really – it is so small it takes time – we haven't time – and to see takes time, like to have a friend takes time."

PRESENT OVER PERFECT

Present is living with your feet firmly grounded in reality, pale and uncertain as it may seem. Present is choosing to believe that your own life is worth investing deeply in, instead of waiting for some rare miracle or fairy tale. Present means we understand that the here and now is sacred, sacramental, threaded through with divinity even in its plainness. Especially in its plainness …

Sink deeply into the world as it stands. Breathe in the smell of rain and scuff of leaves … This is where life is, not in some imaginary, photo-shopped dreamland. Here. Now. You, just as you are. Me, just as I am. This world, just as it is. This is the good stuff. This is the best stuff there is. Perfect has nothing on truly, completely, wide-eyed, open-souled present.

– Shauna Niequist[53]

As I pen this reflection, I'm aware of a number of people whose lives have been turned upside down by the loss of loved ones, a scary medical diagnosis, an unexpected financial crisis, a seemingly unconquerable addiction. For these people and others like them, author Shauna Niequist's praise of the present is anything but inspiring or consoling. For them, and for all of us from time to time, perfect over present would be just fine, thank you.

Fortunately for most of us, the present is usually devoid of life's more difficult challenges; we are often lucky enough to go for long stretches without the trials and tragedies that can wound our bodies and sear our souls. It is these more typically uneventful times that Niequist is inviting us to recognize as potentially replete with meaning, and encouraging us to enter into "completely, wide-eyed," and with an open soul.

So much of our life is spent between the highs and lows that we can easily become lulled and dulled by its predictability. Most of our days and years are spent doing what it takes to sustain ourselves and those in our charge. But those same activities – working, shopping, preparing meals, paying bills, and the like – if we are fully present to them, can become "sacred, sacramental, threaded through with divinity" if we are fully present to them.

Of course, it is not possible to be fully present to the present 24/7, but it is possible to return to the present when we realize that we have become, once again, at a distance from it. Seen in this way, life becomes a matter of returning over and over again to what we are doing and who we are with. This may not sound very exciting, but it might just be the ticket to a more full and fulfilling life.

RELIGIOUS DISTRACTIONS

In my earlier years, the "religious" was for me the exception ... "Religious experience" was the experience of otherness that did not fit into the context of life. Since then, I have given up the "religious" which is nothing but the exception, extraction, exaltation, ecstasy; or it has given me up. I possess nothing but the everyday out of which I am never taken. The mystery has made its dwelling here where everything happens as it happens. I know no fullness but each mortal hour's fullness of claim and responsibility.

– Martin Buber[54]

Jewish mystic and philosopher Martin Buber wrote the words quoted above following a meeting with a student who took his life soon after their encounter. Buber acknowledged being only half present to the young man due to a "religious experience" that left him focused on the life beyond this life. Here he states the radical way he changed upon hearing the tragic news of his student's death – namely, that religion that is not grounded in "each mortal hour's fullness of claim and responsibility" was no longer of interest to him.

Most of us go a lifetime without the kind of "religious experience" that consumed Buber, but we may all be prone to looking for the religious or spiritual dimension of life beyond the demands and duties of everyday life and relationships. God is in heaven, religion is in church, holiness is synonymous with the virtue of saints, and a religious experience is "out of this world." When we fall prey to this sort of thinking, we run the risk of missing not only the sacredness of ordinary life, but the joys, pains, and struggles of the people we encounter every day. If instead we embrace an understanding of God as the Ground of Being, the spiritual essence at the heart of nature and human nature, then being religious becomes a matter of being fully present to wherever we are, whomever we meet, and whatever we do.

Likewise, Jesuit priest, mystic, and paleontologist Teilhard de Chardin reminds us that divinity resides *within* life when he states, "By means of all created things, without exception, the divine assails us, penetrates us, and molds us. We imagine it as distant and inaccessible, whereas in fact we live steeped in its burning layers."[55] Extraordinary experiences can make us aware of a reality beyond life as we know it, but they are a distraction if they cause us to lose touch with the nitty-gritty of life in the world, for "the mystery has made its dwelling here where everything happens as it happens."

SPIRITUAL MATURITY

With spiritual maturity the basis … shifts away from ambition, idealism, and desire for self-transformation. It is as if the wind has changed, and a weather vane – still centered in the same spot – now points in a different direction: back to this

moment. We are no longer striving for a spiritual destination
… We are home. And being home, we sweep the floor, make
nourishing meals, and care for our guests.
— Jack Kornfield[56]

In his book *After the Ecstasy, the Laundry*, psychologist Jack Kornfield makes a case for appreciating the spiritual depth of everyday life. There is a place for "ambition, idealism, and desire for self-transformation" as we strive to become our best selves, but these inner forces can shift our focus away from the responsibilities and relationships that form our often simple and uneventful lives. For Kornfield, spiritual maturity is about realizing the sacredness of those down-to-earth activities required of us on a daily basis.

There is truth in understanding spirituality as more than the concreteness of life as we know it, but the "more" is a dimension *of* rather than something *apart from* what is. Poet and mystic William Blake said, "If the doors of perception were cleansed, everything would appear to man as it is, infinite." If we could see clearly, that is, without the prejudices and presumptions that cloud our vision, we might just catch a glimpse of the sacred nature of life in the world.

The word "appreciation" comes from the two Latin words *ad pretium* meaning "go to the precious." If we penetrate the surface of our work and of our interactions with others, we may discover a preciousness in what might otherwise appear only ordinary and without much value. Sweeping the floor, making nourishing meals, caring for our guests, and other work-related tasks can be a portal, a doorway to the spiritual essence of everything and everyone. When this door opens before us, we are invited to step through it into a new and richer experience of the life we are already living.

THE POWER OF PAUSING

It is the pause in between the chaos that rejuvenates, brings bliss, and makes sense of it all ...
— Amy Jalapeno[57]

Many of us are not only good at what we do, we are good at doing many things at the same time, and doing them at high speeds. We live not only by the adage "the sooner the better," but also "the more the better" and "the faster the better." There is nothing wrong with velocity *per se*, or with being adept at multi-tasking, but living in this manner takes its toll; we become physically worn-out, mentally stressed-out, and emotionally burnt-out. We are people, not machines. When we try to do too much too fast for too long, not only does the quality of our work suffer, but we suffer.

In my work with people seeking spiritual guidance, I often find myself saying that the pace of their lives may be what is keeping them from experiencing the inner peace they desire. I know this to be true because it is the case in my own life. While it can be exhilarating to move from one task to the next, one encounter to another, one demanding responsibility to the one that awaits my attention, doing so often distances me from the realization that I am part of something greater than myself – there is more to me than me!

Pondering the fact that the pace at which I live can be self-defeating, I've come to realize *the power of pausing*. If I just pause mentally between activities, if I just take a deep breath, if I close my eyes and remind myself that I am more than what I am doing, I can feel a shift, a settling, a home-coming of sorts. Blogger Amy Jalapeno (a pseudonym) says it this way: "It is the pause in between the chaos that rejuvenates, brings bliss, and makes sense of it all ... "

There is a space between every activity. There are brief moments between waking up and getting up, between preparing a meal and eating it, between arriving at our destination and getting out of the car, between finishing one task or errand and beginning another. Pausing does not necessarily mean stopping what we're doing. Pausing isn't taking a time out but a "time in" – that is, bringing our consciousness beneath the surface awareness of ourselves to our Sacred Self.

To pause between every activity can be a profound experience. One could call such pauses mini-Sabbaths, for they enable us to get in touch with the divinity of our humanity and the spiritual depth of ordinary life.

THE SACRED IN OUR MIDST

[W]e need to find ways of being reminded that our religious sanctuaries are at best side chapels onto the great cathedral of creation. Otherwise the impression is given ... that God is somehow more present within the four walls than in every other place and that the time for meeting within the four walls of our religious sanctuaries is somehow more sacred than all other moments and that the people who gather within the four walls are somehow more holy than all other people. Tragically, the impression has been created that we seek well-being and salvation by separating ourselves from creation and from the rest of the world rather than by more deeply integrating ourselves.

– J. Philip Newell[58]

Minister and author J. Philip Newell is a proponent of Celtic spirituality, an approach to life and religion that honours the earthy and natural, the relational more than the rational. Its emphasis is on connection not separation, on discovering the holy within life, rather than apart from it.

There has always been a value to the "four walls of our religious sanctuaries," for gathering to worship in a designated place can create a heightened sense of the sacred, one that can be felt as well as believed, one that is more inspirational than institutional, one that creates a sense of community rather than separateness. But such sanctuaries, be they churches, mosques, temples, or synagogues, are, as Newell states, "side chapels onto the great cathedral of creation." All of life, every place, each person, is a venue of the divine – what is missing is our awareness of this life-giving truth.

How different and better might our lives be if we entered our home, our workplace, the mall, grocery store, and bank with the same kind of reverence with which we enter places of worship. If we were to step outside each day breathing in the wonder of creation, the miracle of being alive, wouldn't we be more likely to appreciate what we mostly take for granted? And if we recognized the sacredness of every person, perhaps our relationships might resemble what Jewish philosopher Martin Buber referred to as "I-Thou" encounters.

Of course, this way of being, this constant awareness of the sacred in daily life, is a better way to live. The trick lies in how to remain conscious of it. Nothing short of a daily reminder is necessary if we are to keep the "four walls" from blinding us to the truth expressed by Martin Luther King, Jr. who said, "Church is not the place you come to, it's the place you go from."

WE ARE WAVES ON THE SEA

Much like the life of ordinary waves, we as human beings are gathered in our passion out of a larger home, that sea of infinite spirit, and propelled from an unfathomable depth, we mount and curl and crest and spray, only to subside back into that from which we come.

Profoundly, grace comes to the wave when it realizes what it is made of. Since it has risen from the very same water into which it will crash, its fear of ending is somehow lessened. For it is already a part of where it is going.

Grace comes to the heart when it realizes what it is made of and what it has risen from. In that moment, grace comforts us, that no matter the joy or pain along the way, we are already a part of where we are going.

– Mark Nepo[59]

According to poet Mark Nepo, grace is the experiential re-alization of reassuring peace. Grace is the comforting aware-ness that all is well and will be well because we are never separate from what we are made of; we are always one, both individually and collectively, with the Spirit that enlivens us as we "mount and curl and crest and spray."

Like waves, we are momentary manifestations of the source from which we emerge and to which we will return. We have our own shape and form, our own unique person-ality and physicality, but we come out of a "larger home," a spiritual font that remains often undetected as we go about the day-to-day business of being. In the words of Annie Dillard, we are "a faint tracing on the surface of mystery."[60]

Many of us are afflicted with a kind of spiritual amne-sia, a lack of awareness of our deepest identity – our one-ness with that which is our essence. When in this state of self-estrangement, we are likely to find ourselves aimlessly adrift, relentlessly searching for we know not what. But just as grace comes to the wave when it realizes what it is made of, reassuring peace can come to us when we stop long enough to realize that we are one with the "sea of infinite spirit."

It is no easy task to stop or even to slow the busy pace of our lives. It takes intentionality and discipline to set aside time to breathe in the mystery of our wave-like existence. But unless we make room for grace, our lives will be less than graceful. And unless we make opportunities to recall that we are "a part of where we are going," we will understand death only as the end of life rather than as a homecoming.

WHAT'S NOW?

[F]requently I do drift away from the present by fantasizing about what's coming up next. I now realize that I have spent much of my life thinking about "What's next?" While eating dinner, I will start thinking about what book I am going to read or what movie I am going to watch after dinner. Meantime, I am not focusing on my lovely mouthful of mashed potatoes.

In fact, "What's next?" has been the leitmotif of my life. As a child, I constantly thought about what my life would be when I grew up; later, about what life I would lead when I graduated from college. On and on. Thus have I diluted my life. As Ralph Waldo Emerson wrote, "We are always getting ready to live, but never living."

– Daniel Klein[61]

Having something to look forward to can make our day and our life an adventure. When we can't wait to get up in the morning to tackle the next activity or challenge, life feels full and exciting. But when author Daniel Klein uses the phrase "what's next," he's not talking about looking forward, but overlooking. He's not referring to a full life, but to one that is empty, to the failure to be present to the present. If we are too focused on what's next, we're not likely to experience what's happening now. If our attention is on tomorrow, today can slip away without notice. Annie Dillard writes, "How we spend our days is, of course, how we spend our lives."[62] We may lament the fact that the days pass too quickly, but a more appropriate reason to grieve is that so does life. If we spend our days getting ready to live, we may someday wonder why we never lived.

Because there is often nothing special about today, it is easy to drift into a "what's next" frame of mind. But what a loss it is not to appreciate a "lovely mouthful of mashed potatoes." Life is full of simple delights and minor miracles that, when we enter into them with full awareness and appreciation, can transform how we experience them. So rather than asking what's next, we should perhaps ask "What's now?"

WHAT THE LIVING DO

"What the Living Do" is addressed to her brother, weeks after his death. It begins by detailing a particular morning, one which a person … could easily dismiss as a bad day. The kitchen sink is clogged, and Drano isn't helping. The dishes are piling up. It's cold outside, but the heat in the apartment is cranked up too high … driving a car, carrying a bag of groceries in the street, dropping the bag, spilling coffee, buying a hairbrush. How different all of those seemingly insignificant acts would look if we knew we would never get a chance to do them again.

> *We often hear self-help gurus talk about "living in the moment." And it's true we don't appreciate "what is" nearly enough."*
> — Judith Valente and Charles Reynard[63]

The above quote is taken from a commentary on the poem "What the Living Do" by Marie Howe. My guess is that when we think of poetry most of us do not think of lines that describe a mess in the kitchen and the everyday, often chaotic endeavours that make up our anything but ideal lives. "Dropping the bag" and "spilling coffee" aren't exactly the stuff of poetic gracefulness. But because we usually don't appreciate "what is" until it's too late, it is this element of our existence that Howe wistfully describes in her ode to her deceased brother.

We often tolerate, resent, or take for granted "what is," never pondering "how different all of those seemingly insignificant acts would feel if we knew we would never get a chance to do them again." We look ahead, we plan for the future, we say "see you later" when we part from one another, but we never know if there will be a "later," or if there will be another opportunity to drive a car or buy a hairbrush, or do any of the thousand things we plan to do tomorrow.

We usually engage in everyday acts done automatically. We often undervalue the people with whom we interact. And we ourselves, though only temporary citizens of the earth, are frequently too busy to appreciate the brief and sometimes messy blessing of being alive. There is great wisdom in the simple phrase *memento mori, memento vivere* – "remember death, remember to live." Even dropping a bag of groceries and spilling our coffee doesn't seem so bad when we remember it's only because we are alive that those things can happen.

WONDER-FULL

By and large, our world has lost its sense of wonder. We have grown up. We no longer catch our breath at the sight of a rainbow or the scent of a rose, as we once did. We have grown bigger and everything else smaller, less impressive. We get blasé and worldly-wise and sophisticated. We no longer run our fingers through water, no longer shout at the stars or make faces at the moon. Water is H2O, the stars have been classified ...

There was a time in the not too distant past when a thunderstorm caused grown men to shutter and feel small ... We grow complacent and lead practical lives. We miss the experience of awe, reverence, and wonder.

— Brennan Manning[64]

Former priest and author Brennan Manning names a phenomenon that is all too common in our culture – the tendency to lose the innocence and wonder of youth as we take on the responsibilities that come with age. It is not a necessary loss, it doesn't have to happen, but unless we become intentional about it, we are affected by a gravitational pull that results in our becoming less capable of amazement, less inclined to be smitten by "the sight of a rainbow or the scent of a rose."

"Our birth is but a sleep and a forgetting" says poet William Wordsworth. It is as if we wander the earth in a half-awake haze, a trance-like state that leaves us unable to experience the magical nature of nature, the wonder-filled reality that is creation – and creatures. It is this state of unawareness that is sometimes referred to as "original sin," the imperfection of the human condition.

How can we begin to awake to that which we have become unaware? How can we remember what, in our sophistication, we have forgotten? It is not the mind that will bring us to an appreciation or experience of the sacred depths of nature, ourselves, and others, it is our *senses*. Sensuality is the portal to the soul; earthiness is the doorway to the heavenly in our midst. "I am sensual," claims poet Mary Oliver, "in order to be spiritual."

For many of us, recapturing a sense of wonder requires unlearning the belief that being spiritual necessitates rising above the domain of the ordinary, of the bodily, of the often messy nature of human nature. If we are to experience again a sense of "awe, reverence, and wonder" at the beauty that surrounds us and that is us, we must loosen our grip on a strictly logical, practical, and narrowly religious perception of life.

FOUR

A LIFE-GIVING PERSPECTIVE ON RELIGION

ALTHOUGH IT IS ONE OF THE MOST POWERFUL FORCES FOR GOOD KNOWN TO HU-MANKIND, RELIGION, FOR MANY, HAS CEASED TO BE TRANSFORMATIONAL and has instead become a matter of fulfilling creedal, liturgical, and moral requirements. From the Latin *religare*, meaning to re-bind, religion's beliefs and practices are meant to enhance our relationship with ourselves, with others, and with the God of our understanding. The embers of religion's fast-dying fire stand in need of being fanned into flames that can burn away its dross and rekindle its force for good.

There are ways to interpret religious teachings and beliefs that allow their full spiritual meaning to come alive for us individually and collectively. When we embrace the Spirit and not just the letter of its laws, and when we understand them in a way that speaks to our bodies as well as to our souls, we can be enlivened rather than burdened by religion.

The reflections that make up this section are an attempt to fan the flame – that is, to bring new life to the healing message that religion can offer in the midst of our own and the world's brokenness.

ADVENT: A TIME TO PONDER

During Advent we wait for holiness to come … But Advent waiting is active, not passive. We prepare, consciously and intentionally. Many Christian communities prepare by giving each of the weeks a theme – hope, peace, joy, and love. Such themes express our longing for the God-given energies through which holiness is rooted in the world ... We yearn for hope, peace, joy, and love to be reborn in us.

— Louise Mangan and Nancy Wyse, with Lori Farr[65]

When something is important to us, we do what is necessary to prepare for it. If we have an exam and want to get a good grade, we study. If we have a performance, we rehearse. If we have a game, we practice. If we have a report to write or a presentation to give, we spend time researching. We do what it takes to achieve the outcome we desire.

If they are important to us, this dynamic also applies to religious holy days like Easter and Christmas. Lent is the forty days during which we prepare for the celebration of Easter, and Advent is the four weeks prior to Christmas that is meant to focus our attention on the "reason for the season."

Christmas the holiday is a wonder-filled time of year. Decorating trees, hanging lights, exchanging gifts, and singing carols all create an ambiance that is magical, especially but not only for young children. Christmas the holy day is also magical. Stories about the too-crowded inn, a babe in a manger, and shepherds keeping watch cast a special glow whose warmth can penetrate the hardest heart. But there is a deeper meaning to Christmas than either the secular or even the religious trappings and stories suggest, one that invites us to enter into Advent in a more contemplative manner.

If we view Christmas not merely as history, the celebration of Jesus' birth, but as mystery, the coming of Christ in us, then the weeks prior to December 25 which are so likely to morph into last minute shopping, become a time for stopping. They are not a time to be busy, but a time to be still in the hopeful expectation that a sacred self is forming within us and that we are called to give birth to it.

When we look forward to Christmas, as either a holiday or holy day, we are prone to overlook the God-presence that is our deepest self. Monk and mystic Thomas Merton summons us to recognize that presence in ourselves, and in all humanity: "Make ready for the Christ whose smile, like lightning, sets free the song of everlasting glory that now sleeps in your paper flesh like dynamite." Although our awareness of it is often dormant, there is within each of us a sacredness waiting to be born, a goodness that can bring light to a world shrouded in darkness.

In the midst of the hustle and bustle leading up to Christmas, Advent offers the opportunity to quietly ponder the truth of God's indwelling, to feel its stirrings, and to anticipate its explosive potential to "set free the song of everlasting glory" that waits to be sung through us.

CHRIST BORN IN THEE, IN ME

The people who walked in darkness have seen a great light; those who lived in a land of deep darkness – on them light has shined ... For a child has been born for us, a son given to us; authority rests upon his shoulders; and he is named Wonderful Counselor, Mighty God, Everlasting Father, Prince of Peace.
— Isaiah 9:2, 6

Jesus' followers first celebrated Christmas around the year 150 CE. They chose a day in late December not because it was the actual date of his birth (which is unknown), but because the time of year coincided with the pagan festival of the winter solstice – the beginning of longer days – as a way of proclaiming their belief that with Jesus came the victory of light over darkness, of life over death, of God over gloom.

Radiant though it is, the light of Jesus' presence does not dispel the darkness but instead shines as a beacon of hope, a sign that we are not alone. God is incarnate in our midst no matter how difficult or unfair life may be.

In whom does God dwell now that Jesus is no longer among us in the flesh? Where is the light giving us hope in our darkest days? A 17th-century priest and physician, Angelus Silesius, once said, "If Christ were born a thousand times in Galilee it would be in vain until he were born in thee, in me." Christmas in the fullest, spiritual sense isn't just about history – about Jesus being born, scripture scholars estimate, around 4 BCE in Bethlehem – it is about mystery, God incarnate here and now, "in thee, in me."

The celebration of Christmas is filled with images of a babe in a manger, shepherds, and choirs of angels singing Jesus' praise. This warm and wonderful story easily becomes nostalgic and sentimental if taken literally. When, on the other hand, we realize Christmas is also a celebration of God incarnate "in thee, in me," it becomes a radical invitation to live in a way that bears witness to the presence and power of Love and Light.

No matter what one's beliefs or religious affiliation, if any, Christmas can be a reminder that if our lives are to have meaning, if we are to fulfill our purpose, if this world is to become the "Kin-dom" (web of loving relationships) it is meant to be, we must be people through whom "a light has shone."

BLESSED BLUR

[P]eople say it is presumptive to claim I am God, whereas it is an expression of great humility. That man who says "I am the

*slave of God" affirms two existences, his own and God's. But he
that says, "I am God" has made himself non-existent and has
given himself up and says, "I am God, I am naught, He
is all, there is no being but God's." This is the extreme of
humility ...*

— Rumi[66]

Jelaluddin Rumi was a Muslim mystic who lived in the 13th
century in what is now present-day Turkey. Although this
sentiment strikes the Western ear as nothing less than heretical, the same thinking is present in every religious and spiritual tradition including Judeo-Christianity. Some examples:

"You are part of God. All is one, there is no duality, no 'I
and Thou,' God and myself" (William Johnston, SJ).

"God's being is my being ... wherever I am, there is God"
(Meister Eckhart).

"God is the life of your life" (St. Augustine).

"There is a union of God's spirit and our inner-most
self, so that we and God are in all truth one spirit" (Thomas
Merton).

This is not the message most of us received in our religious upbringing. Speaking for myself, I was always taught
that the line between humanity and divinity was clear and
distinct; God was a Supreme Being, and we were not. But
exposure to the teachings of the mystics has led me to realize that that line is really a blessed blur, or as spiritual teacher
James Finley puts it, "We are not God, but we are not other
than God, either."[67] Like the ocean and water, or flame and
fire, humanity and divinity are not separate entities, but dimensions of one vast, spiritual Mystery.

All of this can be a matter of the mind, ideas, and concepts about which we can agree or disagree. However, the
teachings of the mystics are not concerns of the head but of

the heart. They are not about speculation, but about participation, that is, living with reverence, passion, and compassion based on the belief that God by whatever name is enfleshed – in us *as* us.

The union of humanity and divinity calls us to care for and about everyone, but especially those on the margins of society, for as one Jewish mystic put it, "whatever you did for one of the least of these brothers and sisters of mine, you did for me" (Matthew 25:40, NIV).

THE BIRTH OF JESUS, THE COMING OF THE CHRIST

Make ready for the Christ whose smile like lightning sets free the song of everlasting glory that now sleeps in your paper flesh like dynamite.

– Thomas Merton[68]

These simple but explosive words from monk and mystic Thomas Merton convey the spiritual meaning of Advent, the four-week period before Christmas, when Christians are encouraged to prepare for the celebration of Jesus' birth. But there is another equally important understanding of Advent that has to do with the coming of Christ in and through us.

"Christ" is a Greek word that means "anointed" or "anointed one." This designation refers to a person who is called to perform a sacred charge, one chosen for a spiritual endeavour. It is certainly an appropriate term to use in reference to Jesus, for by embodying and proclaiming the unconditional love of Yahweh his mission was to bring healing and hope, mercy and compassion, peace and justice, to Jews and Gentiles alike.

But "Christ" is also a word that applies to all of us no matter what our religious affiliation – if any. There is a "song of everlasting glory" longing to be sung through us, a dormant spiritual presence to which we are called to give birth. Call it soul, true self, or psyche, there is within each of us a sacred self waiting to emerge so that our darkened world might become a better, brighter place. For some this involves extraordinary efforts to bring about systemic change; for most of us it means committing random acts of kindness every day.

When viewed in this manner, both Advent and Christmas become more real, more vital, more immediate. We are not talking about preparing for something that happened in a faraway place over 2,000 years ago, but for a reality that needs to happen *here* and *now* if we are to experience a sense of meaning, purpose, and fulfillment for ourselves, and healing for our broken world.

RELENT FOR LENT

> *There was a time when meadow, grove, and stream*
> *The earth, and every common sight,*
> *To me did seem*
> *Appareled in celestial light,*
> *The glory and the freshness of a dream.*
> *It is not now as it hath been of yore; –*
> *Turn whereso'er I may,*
> *By night or day,*
> *The things which I have seen I now can see no more.*
> – William Wordsworth[69]

In this excerpt from his opus "Intimations of Immortality," poet William Wordsworth describes a time of blissful newness, harmony, and innocence that is our birthright. It is the Garden of Eden, that mythical paradise which we no longer inhabit. After eating the proverbial apple, Adam and Eve head for the exit, mistakenly believing that God is angry at them when in fact, God wanted only to embrace them and welcome them back.

Being a myth, this story describes a reality that is forever true. Having inherited Adam and Eve's original sin – of giving in to the temptation to believe that they were somehow insufficient and needed to be more God-like – we, too, often believe we must achieve an unattainable level of virtue, perfection, or holiness in order to be worthy in God's eyes. And because we do not usually measure up to the divine standards of approval we create in our minds, we mistakenly assume we are a disappointment and are thus not deserving of unconditional love.

What does this have to do with Lent you might ask? Lent has traditionally been a time when we forgo things we enjoy for the 40 days prior to Easter in favour of repentance and disciplines such as prayer, fasting, and almsgiving – the idea being that by doing these things we will please or appease God and earn our way to that other "Garden," heaven. But along with whatever forms of discipline we may choose to engage in, we might also think of Lent as a time to *relent*, that is, to cease resisting the God-love that we think we must earn and, instead, humbly accept the love that is ours. In this case, Lent would be a time to go from fast to slow, from running to resting, from noisy to quiet, from being scattered to mindful, from giving up what we enjoy to giving in to being loved.

If, as a Lenten practice, we were to sit in quiet receptivity to unconditional love for 40 seconds three times a day (morning, noon, and night), Lent might become a time of transformation, one that could enable us to see and experience life, others, and ourselves "appareled in celestial light."

EASTER: HISTORY AND MYSTERY

Awaken, you buried seeds asleep in your earthen tombs.
Rise up with joy to break forth the hard coffins of your shells.
Your Easter time has come; the song of the dove is heard over
the softening land.
Winter has hidden, and spring now dances on your graves to
waken the dead.
Awaken, seeds of holiness buried deep within me.
Rise up to fulfill your destiny whose time has come.
For sanctity is scribbled bold within my blood and brain.
Onward and beyond have I been called even before I felt
the sun or knew the earth around me.
May spring enchant the saint, shy and hesitant within me
and set the rhythm for my sluggish feet in a dance of holy
yearning.

— Ed Hayes[70]

It may come as a surprise, but Christians do not believe Jesus rose from the dead! Contrary to popular opinion he did not sit up, dust himself off, and walk out of the tomb on his own. The true Christian teaching is that Jesus was *raised* from the dead. The Spirit that enlivened him throughout his life was not defeated by death but was a tangible presence his followers experienced even after he died.

In his poem "A Seed Psalm," Father Ed Hayes claims that the same life source that breathed in Jesus breathes in every person, you and me included. The reality of the Spirit's presence in us has to do with the fact that "sanctity is scribbled bold within my blood and brain." There is a spiritual component to our DNA no matter what our religious beliefs, if any. And because the Spirit is at the heart of us, we are urged from within to emerge from the graves that entomb us, the half-alive way we too often go about our days and our lives: "shy and hesitant" and with "sluggish feet."

A seed buried in the earth has within it the drive to become alive. So it was with Jesus and is with us. Death may be the end of our physical existence, but what is most essential lives on.

EVERYBODY WORSHIPS

In the day-to-day trenches of adult life, there is actually no such thing as atheism. There is no such thing as not worshipping. Everybody worships. The only choice we get is what to worship. And an outstanding reason for choosing some sort of god or spiritual-type thing ... is that pretty much anything else you worship will eat you alive. If you worship money and things ... then you will never have enough ... Worship your own body and beauty and sexual allure and you will always feel ugly, and when time and age starts showing, you will die a million deaths before they finally plant you ... Worship power – you will feel weak and afraid ... Worship your intellect, being seen as smart – you will end up feeling stupid, a fraud, always on the verge of being found out.

– David Foster Wallace[71]

Worship is a word we typically associate with religion, with honouring a deity by saying prayers, singing hymns, and reading scripture in "places of worship." But in his 2005 commencement address at Kenyon College, author David Foster Wallace puts worship in a broader context. Wallace implies that we worship something when we give it the power to define us, to be the measure of our worth, to be that which we pursue in order to feel successful, secure, fulfilled, and worthwhile.

In his advice to young graduates, Wallace is making a case for worshipping "some sort of god or spiritual-type thing" because anything less will "eat you alive." When we worship at the altar of false gods, we judge ourselves and others by that which is temporal and temporary. There is nothing inherently evil about money, material possessions, bodies, power, intellect, and the like, but because they are finite, they can never satisfy an infinite longing; because they are not a "spiritual-type thing," they cannot satisfy a spiritual need. If we attempt to find ultimate meaning in what is less than ultimate, we will feel chronically unfulfilled.

It can be difficult to discern whether something or someone we value has become an object of worship. One indication that we have crossed a line is if we feel driven, obsessed, and insecure about where we invest our time and energy. The haunting sense of "never enough-ness" is another sure sign that we are worshipping a false god. British playwright George Bernard Shaw referred to this sense of insufficiency when he said, "There are two great disappointments in life: one is not to get one's heart's desire, and the other is to get it!"

Perhaps we would do well to pursue not the desire of our heart, but of our soul; not that which makes us happy, but that which can bring us joy; not that which will end, but that which has lasting value – unless, that is, you don't mind being eaten alive!

EVERYDAY MIRACLES

28 seconds … the crowd going insane … Kharlamov shooting into the American end again … McClanahan is there … the puck is still loose … 11 seconds! You've got 10 seconds! Countdown going on right now! … Morrow up to Silk … Five seconds left in the game! … DO YOU BELIEVE IN MIRACLES? YES! (Al Michaels, sportscaster)

People say to me all the time, "I remember exactly where I was when I saw the Miracle on Ice." Usually when people say something like that, they're talking about a tragedy. "I remember where I was on September 11." "I remember where I was when I heard the space shuttle had exploded." But this was a positive moment – not just in sports history, but American history.

– Dan Brooks (coach's son)[72]

The "Miracle on Ice" was the against-all-odds victory of the American hockey team over the heavily favoured team from the Soviet Union in the 1980 Winter Olympics. Twenty-nine years later, another "miracle" happened, one that took place not on ice but on water. It was on New York City's Hudson River that Captain Chesley "Sully" Sullenberger landed a disabled plane full of passengers with no fatalities – an occurrence that became known as "The Miracle on the Hudson." Every day we see evidence of the "miracle of modern medicine" when health care professionals ply their trade with the help of medication and technology that was unheard of just a short time ago.

What these and other miracles have in common is that they are not the kind of magic with which the word "miracle" is often associated. They are not the result of heavenly intervention. These miracles were and are the product of hard work, intense training, skilled execution, and perhaps a good bit of holy luck. This is not to say that the "hand of God" is not involved when amazing things take place. Rather, it is an acknowledgement of the fact that the spiritual presence to which the word "God" refers most often works not apart from our efforts, but through them.

"Pray to God and row like hell for shore" is a saying that speaks to this truth. When faced with daunting tasks, it is natural to call upon a presence or strength or power that we may believe will move and guide us safely and effectively, but the work is ours to do. In his own down-to-earth way, humorist and philosopher Mark Twain said something that tangentially applies: "Opportunity is often missed because it's dressed in overalls and looks like work."

We may miss the opportunity to see miracles if we understand them only as instances of divine intervention rather than the result of divinity's yeast-like presence. The unlikely victory, the unbelievable outcome, the evolution of knowledge and skill are all everyday miracles in their own amazing, wonderful, often subtle, embedded in the human way.

FIRST-HAND RELIGION

I have been a God-guy virtually all my life. You might say that was inevitable, being raised in the context of conservative white American Christianity as I was. I was singing Bible songs and memorizing Bible verses before I could read. My skinny boyhood butt sat in a well-padded church pew two or three times a week. On Friday nights I went to Bible club, and in the summers I went to Bible camp. My dad led the family in Bible reading and family devotions almost every night at dinner. One way or another, a religious upbringing like that makes an impression.

— Brian McLaren[73]

Like pastor and author Brian McLaren, many of us have been God-guys and girls since our youth; we have been influenced from earliest times by the religious attitudes and opinions of our elders. But even if our religious upbringing was less intense than his, it's a pretty safe bet that what we learned has had a significant impact on our lives.

McLaren has become famous, or infamous depending on your outlook, for having outgrown much of what he once held to be unquestionably true. He has given himself permission to honour what he has learned through education and experience that is inconsistent with his former beliefs. He has "thrown out the baby and kept the bathwater" – rejected some specific beliefs but held on to the spiritual essence of his faith tradition.

Whether it was the Bible, the Koran, the Torah, or the scripture of any other faith tradition that formed our early impressions of matters religious, it is important to maintain an open mind and heart when it comes to what we have learned. Openness enables growth and counters stagnation; it allows for dialogue and resists judgment. What is often the case, however, is that in the realm of religion what is mistaken for faith is to remain steadfast and unchanging, to believe what we were taught from womb to tomb.

Philosopher William James coined the phrase "secondhand religion" when referring to the beliefs that have been handed on from others. And psychiatrist Gerald May makes the distinction between tradition and traditionalism – the former being the living faith of the dead, while the latter is the dead faith of the living. For James, for May, and perhaps for us as well, what is important is not merely believing what we were taught, but making those beliefs our own by grappling, doubting, questioning, and, possibly even rejecting them when we need to do so for the sake of our own spiritual and intellectual integrity.

Although religion has been at the heart of many conflicts interpersonally and internationally, it has been a positive force for good throughout human history. But in the last analysis, the purpose of religious teachings is not merely to believe them, but to *live* them, not to use them to distinguish ourselves from others, but to find in them the common spiritual bond that unites us to all peoples.

FROM FEAR TO FAITH

Everybody's got fear. Everybody's afraid something bad is going to happen sometime. That's life. But what's important is that you don't let it stop you from doing things, taking risks. Every decision is a risk, every choice leaves a choice behind. You can't let yourself get paralyzed by the fear of what might go wrong.

You have to appreciate people who struggle to overcome their fears. Jimmy Piersall was a real good player for the Red Sox, but he had a nervous breakdown because he had all sorts of paranoid fears – they even made a movie about him called **Fear Strikes Out.** *The good thing was that Jimmy eventually got better, got his confidence back, and played a great centerfield. He always stayed a bit flaky, though. How many guys used to take bug spray to the outfield?*

— Yogi Berra[74]

Along with having been one of the truly outstanding players in the game, Yogi Berra is remembered for his wit, wisdom, and a down-to-earth way of simply saying simple truths. And he was right when he said, "everybody's got fear."

It's been said that humans are born with two fears: falling and loud noises. Every other fear is learned. If that is true, we've done a pretty good job of learning! We've learned, among other things, to be afraid of failure, death, heights, the dark, the unknown, rejection, and sadly, each other – especially when the "other" doesn't look, believe, or think like we do.

"Every decision is a risk, every choice leaves a choice behind." Because our learned fears impact the decisions and choices we make, they often prevent us from taking the risks that bring about growth. Mythologist Joseph Campbell says *the cave you fear to enter holds the treasure you seek*. The deep sense of joy, peace, and aliveness we long for is the treasure we seek whether we know it or not. These conditions of the soul can be experienced only if we do not allow our fears to keep us from venturing into the "places" we are afraid to enter.

Yogi Berra said Jimmy Piersall got better because he got his confidence back. The word "confidence" is derived from the Latin *con fides*, which means "with faith." Faith, be it in God, our self, or life itself, is what enables us to override fear. Faith is a matter of entrusting ourselves to what is beyond or deep within us, with the assurance *not* that all will be well but that acting in the face of fear is itself a good thing – no matter what the outcome.

Because faith does not necessarily dispel fear, and despite the fact that it may seem a bit flaky, it's okay to bring some bug spray into the cave!

GOD: PERSON OR PRESENCE

A pious old man prayed five times a day while his business partner never set foot in church. And now, on his eightieth birthday he prayed thus:

Oh Lord our God! Since I was a youth, not a day have I allowed to pass without coming to church in the morning and saying my prayers … Not a single move, not one decision, important or trifling, did I make without first invoking your Name. And now, in my old age, I have doubled my exercises of piety and pray to you ceaselessly, night and day. Yet here I am, poor as a church mouse. But look at my business partner. He drinks and gambles and, even at his advanced age, consorts with women of questionable character, yet he's rolling in wealth … Why, why, why have you let him prosper and why do you treat me thus?" "Because," said God in reply, "you are such a monumental bore!"

– Anthony DeMello[75]

I bet you were surprised by the punch line of this story – I know I was! According to conventional thinking, God is supposed to be someone who is pleased with a pious person, not bored; happier with someone who *prays* than with someone who *plays*. My guess is that the intention of the storyteller, Jesuit priest Anthony DeMello, is not merely to surprise, but to confound us, to cause us to ponder our assumptions about religious matters.

The bigger question here, however, is not whether God is someone who is bored or pleased by our actions, but whether God is anyone at all. It is human nature to imagine that God is a better version of our selves – a loving, forgiving, parent-like figure with whom we can win points by being on our best behaviour. However, it might just be that when we imagine God in this manner we limit that which is limitless. The mystics of all religious traditions posit that the word "God" does not refer to a person, but to the spiritual essence of life; to a force for good; to a benevolent, enveloping Presence. This may strike some as New Age thinking, but it is actually age-old wisdom that is found in ancient Christian writings such as the Acts of the Apostles, where we find the statement "In God we live and move and have our being" (Acts 17:28).

For most people it is important to hold fast to a conventional notion of the divine, for it gives them purpose and direction in the maze-like journey through life. But many others find it difficult to embrace theism, the idea that God is a Supreme Being who intervenes from time to time, but who is essentially apart from creation. While some of these reject belief in God altogether, others have come to affirm God as the spiritual "ground of being," to use theologian Paul Tillich's term. Wherever we land in this regard, whether the divine is for us a person or a presence, I hope that none of us is considered a "monumental bore"!

GRACE BATS LAST

Amazing grace how sweet the sound that saved a wretch like me.
I once was lost but now I'm found was blind but now I see.
'Twas grace that taught my heart to fear, and grace my fears relieved.
How precious did that grace appear the hour I first believed.
Through many dangers toils and snares we have already come.
'Twas grace that brought us safe thus far and grace will lead us home.
When we've been there ten thousand years bright shining as the sun.
We've no less days to sing God's praise than when we'd first begun.

— John Henry Newton

Is there a person on the planet who has not heard this song? Is there a singer who hasn't sung it? Is there anyone who does not resonate with its truth? The words are those of John Newton, a slave trader who was lost in and blind to the evil he perpetrated, until one day, after a near-death experience at sea, he saw the light and changed his ways.

It's often the case, that we need a wake-up call in order to see that we've gone off course, lost our way, become someone we don't recognize and may not like very much. Without realizing it, we can drift from "true north," wander from the innocence that used to be who we used to be. Our faults may not be as glaring as those of John Newton, but the subtle sense of not-rightness that may visit us from time to time can be unsettling.

"Amazing grace how sweet the sound that saved a wretch like me." Being "saved" is not merely a matter of being made aware of and rescued from our wayward ways, but of finding and seeing within ourselves a Presence we have lost touch with, one that holds and enfolds us no matter how far astray we may have wandered. We easily forget that there is an infinite and benevolent Spirit in whose proverbial eye we are the apple on our worst, as well as our best days. This is what is so amazing about this grace-presence, it is unconditional, it is invincible, it is sovereign, persistent, and unrelenting. When we forget this truth, we may feel lost and blind, we can feel like it's game over – but *grace bats last!*

In his book *The Contemplative Heart*, psychologist James Finley says it this way: "Grace amazes us not by resolving … our forgetfulness, but by dissolving it in a love that lays bare the preciousness of ourselves in our forgetfulness."[76] In other words, our "wretchedness" may not be the result of our having lost our way, but of our thinking that losing our way means that we are less than treasured, cherished, prized, and precious. Grace is the "walk off" hit, the game winning reminder that although we may forget, we're never forgotten, and even though we may be blind, we are always seen through loving eyes.

IN PRAISE OF IRREVERENCE

*The chief rabbi of the shtetl (small Jewish town), a sage
renowned throughout the land as the greatest mind in Jewish
thought, is approached by two young Seekers of Truth. They
have traveled for weeks, a great distance, on foot, in order to sit
at his feet.*

*"Rabbi," asks one, eager for wisdom. "Why can't we eat
pork?"*

*The Rabbi reels back and, smacking his hand to his
forehead, exclaims, "We can't? Uh-oh!"*
   – David Rakoff[77]

Award winning author and self-proclaimed curmudgeon
David Rakoff pokes fun at his Jewish religion with this story
of a rabbi who should know that a good Jew doesn't eat pork.
Using humour to make his point, Rakoff proclaims the importance of not taking religious rules too seriously.

Perhaps the rabbi was truly wise and not surprised by
the censure against eating pork, but knowing his question-
ers were expecting a wise and learned response to their
inquiry, and that they were confined by a legalistic understanding of Judaism, his intent was to shock them into a
different and more liberating way of thinking. This may
also be the point of the iconoclastic Buddhist saying, "What
did the master say to the hot dog vender? Make me one
with everything!" And it may have been the impact Jesus
wanted to have on his followers when he, despite its being
forbidden, performed healings on the Sabbath; when he
told parables with unlikely heroes (the Good Samaritan);
and when he paradoxically claimed that the last shall be
first and the greatest serves the rest.

Whether in the realm of religion or any other aspect of life, we can easily become rigid in our understanding about how we are to live. Without intending to do so, we can find ourselves thinking, believing, and acting small about matters that are boundless, contenting ourselves with keeping the letter of the law rather than living its spirit.

We can experience a reassuring sense of security and comfort when we comply with conventional ways of living, but like the "Seekers of Truth" in Rakoff's story, we may sometimes need a wake-up call, we may have to be shocked, have the rug pulled out from under us, or be blindsided by a larger truth in order to become more fully alive.

LOOKING FOR HOME

William James distinguished between what he called the once-born and the twice-born. The once-born are those who do not question existence and live out their lives with contentment. They are at home in themselves and in the world because they do not wonder why. It's as if someone gave them a happiness gene. The twice-born are aware of their failings and the sufferings of life, and they long for a harmony that seems unattainable in this world. Unsatisfied with the palliatives that the world can offer — wealth, fame, success, a beautiful mind or body — and all too conscious of their failings and vulnerabilities, they set out on their own journey of self-discovery, only to realize finally that what they are looking for has been there all along. They have been looking for home.

— Roger Housden[78]

The term "born again" is usually associated with Christians who have accepted Jesus as their "personal saviour," those who consider themselves "saved" and who take it upon themselves to evangelize those who, in their opinion, are not. To be born again is to be reborn into beliefs that bring certitude and security about life here and hereafter. When philosopher and psychologist William James uses the term "twice-born," he is not referring to people who have found certitude or security, but to those who do a double take with regard to life, who ponder its meaning and question their purpose.

The thought of being "once-born" is compelling, for who would not want to be "at home in themselves and in the world," content with the "palliatives that the world can offer," and the recipient of a "happiness gene"? But in the realm of both religion and psychology, to be born once does not make us fully alive. When we unthinkingly buy into the ethos of our religious or secular culture, when we settle for keeping the rules of our faith tradition or for striving after perishable goods and goals, something in us remains unfulfilled.

The Greek thinker Socrates is often quoted as saying "the unexamined life is not worth living." To be "twice-born" means we examine both ourselves and life. It means we question why things are the way they are in an attempt to improve ourselves and our world. James states that the "twice-born" are looking for home, something poet Robert Frost defined as the place where, when you go there, they have to let you in. The examined life is a journey of self-discovery that leads to the realization that the home, the harmony, meaning, belonging, and fulfillment we seek is here, woven into the fabric of our daily duties and relationships.

NEW AGE OR AGE OLD?

You can live your own little life as "you" or you can surrender to the source of who you really are – your soul. It is in that realm that real greatness, magic, and miracles happen. This is the Gandhi zone, the Jesus zone. It's a level of consciousness that the miracle makers of our world are living in.

When you surrender, that is when the big magic happens ... What if you could live life that way? Living in a state where you are always alert to what may be seeking to happen through you, instead of asking why things aren't happening. A state where you have let go of the way things should happen and stand openhandedly ready to receive whatever is coming.

— Kute Blackson[79]

This quote from author and inspirational speaker Kute Blackson sounds a little like psycho-spiritual babble to me. His use of the phrase "a level of consciousness," and the words "zone," "miracles," and "magic," makes me a little skeptical that there is any real depth to the surrender he's advocating. But the possibility of being locked into a way of thinking and acting that is vital, alive, and energetic is attractive to say the least.

Perhaps it is only a thin line that separates New Age thinking from age old wisdom. It may be just a matter of semantics that distinguishes one from the other, for like the "zone" referred to by Blackson, the teachings and traditions of most mainline religions invite their adherents to experience life fully, freely, and forcefully. At their best, religious teachings encourage passion, not passivity; they promote letting go of control and the willingness to follow the lead of the Spirit. This is faith at its best – yielding, trusting, "openhandedly ready to receive whatever is coming."

In a desire to conform to religious teachings, we can easily lose sight of their invitation to live not just according to the letter of the law, but to its spirit. When the former becomes our *modus operandi*, we end up with a "little life," one whose focus is on keeping our scorecard clean in the eyes of

God. A more soulful way to live, one that resembles the "Gandhi zone, the Jesus zone," is articulated by journalist Hunter Thompson who wrote, "Life should not be a journey to the grave with the intention of arriving safely in a pretty and well-preserved body, but rather to skid in broadside in a cloud of smoke, thoroughly used up, totally worn out, and loudly proclaiming: 'Wow! What a Ride!'"[80]

ON FIRE

Abbot Lot came to Abbot Joseph and said: "Father, according as I am able, I keep my little rule, and my little fast, my prayer, meditations and contemplative silence; and according as I am able I strive to cleanse my heart of thoughts: now what more should I do?" The elder rose up in reply and stretched out his hands to heaven, and his fingers became like ten lamps of fire. He said: "Why not be totally changed into fire?"

— Thomas Merton[81]

This story comes from the tradition of the Desert Fathers and Mothers, third-century CE ascetical men and women who sought refuge from the world; men and women who embraced a life of radical simplicity and solitude in order to fully dedicate themselves to God.

Like many who are sincere about their religion, Abbot Lot fell prey to striving for perfection by practicing his "little rule" and "little fast." He wanted to be a good monk and to do all the right things in the right ways, but in doing so his life became small and self-focused. Because he was a wise mentor, Abbot Joseph recognized Lot's misguided zeal and invited him to be "changed into fire," that is, to be consumed with God rather than being obsessed with his own devotional practices.

We are all prone to becoming self-focused when we desire to improve ourselves. Whether in the realm of religion, work, relationships, or any other aspect of life, it is easy to set our sights too low. Getting better at living our faith, more capable and knowledgeable about our job, or more loving as a partner, parent, or friend are noble endeavours, but to content ourselves with achieving these goals may render us less than we are capable of becoming and other than who we are called to be.

"Why not be totally changed into fire?" Why not surrender ourselves to the Spirit that, in the words of monk and mystic Thomas Merton, sleeps in our paper flesh like dynamite? Why not let go of our striving to merely improve ourselves and instead join forces with a Higher or Inner Power – one that enables us to overcome the temptation to only act "according as I am able" and instead inspires us to become more than we ever imagined? If we do so, if we open our minds and hearts to the God of our understanding, we may find that what inhabits us is stronger than what inhibits us.

THE HOUND OF HEAVEN

Adam hid in the Garden of Eden. Moses tried to substitute his brother. Jonah jumped a boat and was swallowed by a whale. Man likes to run from God. It's a tradition. So perhaps I was only following tradition when as soon as I could walk, I started running ... by the time I graduated (from college) and went out into the world, I was as well versed in my religion as any secular man I knew.

And then?

And then I pretty much walked away from it.

It wasn't revolt. It wasn't some tragic loss of faith. It was, if

I'm being honest, apathy ... I attended no service. Who had time? I was fine. I was healthy. I was making money. I was climbing the ladder. I didn't need to ask God for much, and I figure, as long as I wasn't hurting anyone, God wasn't asking much of me either. We had forged a sort of you go your way, I'll go mine arrangement. At least in my mind.

– Mitch Albom[82]

Author and columnist Mitch Albom is nothing if not honest in his religious self-assessment. Jewish by birth, Albom was too afraid in his childhood, and too busy as a young adult, to open his heart to God. Like so many others, he turned his back on formal religion but found that he was unable and eventually uninterested in outrunning the God who dwells within.

The instinct to follow the "tradition" is powerful. One person who knew this to be true and who gave poetic voice to it was Francis Thompson. In his work "The Hound of Heaven," he wrote, "I fled him down the nights and down the days. I fled him down the arches of the years. I fled him down the labyrinthine ways of my own mind, and in the mist of tears." The instinct to run notwithstanding, Albom, and Thompson before him, found that the spiritual connection to the divine within is a different animal than obedience to the God of institutional religious beliefs and practices. It is the bond with the divine *within* that matters most, and that is ultimately impossible to outrun.

We live in an era that is increasingly a-religious, but we also exist at a time characterized by an intense spiritual hunger. Although we often experience this hunger as a desire for material and relational fulfillment, it is really the "hound of heaven" nipping at our heels, inviting us not to run but to rest in the divine.

THE ONE GOD

I am in love
with every church
and mosque
and temple
and any kind of shrine
because I know it is there
that people say the different names
of the one God.
—Hafiz[83]

These beautifully inclusive words are the work of Hafiz, a 14th-century Persian poet and spiritual teacher. They were as radical in his day as they are in ours, and just as important to embrace. Our theologies may differ and our religions may be diverse, but there is only one ultimate, intimate reality at their core, one Spirit that weaves through their diversity and our humanity.

Hafiz is not only the name of a person, it is also a word that refers to one who has memorized the Koran. This could, of course, apply to any scripture. There is a difference between memorization and knowing something "by heart." The former is a matter of the mind and is about remembering, while the latter is a matter of the whole person, and is about re-membering. The latter is the meaning to which the word "hafiz" applies.

When we re-member, we open ourselves to a relationship with the truth of the words we read, and we are impacted by them. There is a story about a student who went to his rabbi saying excitedly, "Rabbi, I have gone through the Torah" (the first five books of the Old Testament). When the rabbi ignored him, the student said it again with even more emotion: "Rabbi, I've gone through the Torah." Again the rabbi was dismissive. After being approached a third time by his eager student, the rabbi simply said, "Yes, I know, you've gone through the Torah, but has the Torah gone through you?"

Hafiz says, "Fear is the cheapest room in the house. I would like to see you living in better conditions." If we remember the words of holy books, if we allow them to go through us, we move beyond the fear that often prevents us from recognizing the truth celebrated in every church, mosque, temple, and shrine – that there are different names for the one God.

THE ORDER IS LOVE

Were one asked to characterize the life of religion in the broadest and most general terms possible, one might say that it consists of the belief that there is an unseen order, and that our supreme good lies in harmoniously adjusting ourselves thereto. This belief and this adjustment are the religious attitude in the soul.

– William James[84]

In his classic work *Varieties of Religious Experience*, physician, philosopher, and psychologist William James makes the case for a broader understanding of religion than is commonly held. Most of us are likely to think of religion in terms of the 3 Cs: creed (beliefs), cult (worship), and code (morality), which are elements of every mainline religious tradition. Religion thus understood is something we do, or practice; it is a set of beliefs and requirements meant to keep us on the proverbial "straight and narrow" road that leads to heaven. When embraced with an open mind and heart, this brand of religion can be a powerful source and force for good, but when held to literally and from a fundamentalist mindset, it has often led to conflict and even to wars.

For a growing number of people, a religion of requirements has ceased to have meaning. For some, their disaffection is merely a rebellion against the demands of their faith tradition, but many others – young and old alike – are genuinely seeking a sense of connection with something ultimate and infinite that they have not found in institutional religion. The renowned architect Frank Lloyd Wright counted himself among this population when he said, "I believe in God, only I spell it Nature." And controversial comedian Lenny Bruce spoke for this group when he said that people are straying away from church and going back to God!

From the Latin *re ligare* (re-bind), true religion is about relationship, connection, and harmony with an "unseen order." There is, both within and beyond us, a spiritual Presence which, when we are attuned to it, results in our living virtuously, for *ordo est amor*, "the order is Love." This understanding of religion is what James refers to as an "attitude in the soul," It is an attitude that may resonate with those who do not consider themselves religious in a conventional sense, for connection to the ultimate and infinite leads not to conflict and war, but to a sense of community based on the sacredness of every person.

TURNING HERE INTO HEAVEN

In mainstream religious traditions, a creator may be ostensibly worshipped while the creation itself is dishonored; our Western political system and economy are rife with people who claim, for example, allegiance with Judeo-Christian religions yet do not flinch at profiting from the destruction of Earth's life support systems. Reverence is reserved for a disembodied god, or for an afterlife, while the physical universe – the creation itself – is largely regarded as inanimate, dead, a warehouse of senseless objects for exploitation and consumption.

– Geneen Marie Haugen[85]

As we find ourselves in the midst of a climate crisis, environmentalist and scholar Geneen Marie Haugen challenges our religious, political, and economic systems to recognize the sacredness of nature, the God-infused character of creation, and the holiness of the universe and of the tiny planet that sustains our existence. Haugen's message is therefore important and timely. Her perspective on this crisis invites us to look closely at our understanding of God and what it means to be religious.

As she points out, many of us have been raised to believe that God is a being separate from creation, and to relegate "Him" to the heavens. What sometimes follows from this view is the tendency to undervalue life in the here and now, and to focus on the afterlife – the reward or punishment that may await us when we die. When we fall prey to this way of thinking, religion becomes a matter of pleasing and appeasing a distant God, rather than being in relationship with the presence of the divine hidden in plain sight, cloaked in the ordinary and often mundane reality of our everyday life. Author and farmer Wendell Berry views the notion of a distant God as disastrous: "Perhaps the greatest disaster of human history is one that happened to or within religion: that is the conceptual division between the holy and the world, the excerpting of the Creator from creation."[86]

Our failure to sense the spiritual depth of creation and of our daily lives can result in a loss of meaning, a "why bother" attitude that may border on depression. An anti-dote to these feelings that can lead to both self-care and care of the earth is the realization that the word "God" does not necessarily refer to a Supreme Being but to that dimension of reality theologian Paul Tillich referred to as the "ground of being," the hallowed essence at the heart of life. This understanding of God makes being religious not merely a matter of believing and worshipping, but of rolling up our sleeves and doing our part to turn "here" into heaven.

FIVE

DISCOVERING HOLINESS WITHIN

Abide Inside
A Path with Heart
Avoiding the Void
Beautifully Fragile
Crossing a Threshold
Discovering Our Sacred Self
Heeding the Voiceless Voice
Homeless No More
It's Hard on the Soul
Life within Life
Love and Laugh
Pessimism/Optimism
Querencia
Resting in Our Soul
Seeking Sanctuary
Self-Care First
Spot of Grace
That I May See
The Gift of Loneliness
Touching a Soul

DIPLOMAT AND MYSTIC DAG HAMMARSKJÖLD SAID, "THERE IS WITHIN EACH OF US A STILL POINT SURROUNDED BY SILENCE." There is a sacred centre, a soul dimension to our selves that makes the distinction between humanity and divinity a blessed blur. We are not God, but we are not other than God either.

But like stones skipping across a pond, many of us tend to live apart from our spiritual depths as we skim the surface of life. While moving from one endeavour to another, one person to the next, one task, project, and venture to what awaits our attention, we are inclined to identify with our ego, the physical, mental, emotional dimensions of ourselves, but remain out of touch with our soul.

Because we are prone to forgetting that we are a Sacred Self, the following reflections are intended to remind us of that truth, and to appreciate that what is true of each of us is true of all of us.

ABIDE INSIDE

Co-dependence is the most common of all addictions: the addiction to looking elsewhere. We believe that something outside of ourselves ... can give us happiness or fulfillment. The "elsewhere" may be people, places, things, behaviors or experiences ...

One of the reasons for our being is to get to know ourselves in a deeper, richer, and more profound way. We can do that

only if we are truly in relationship with our selves, with others, and with the God of our understanding.
— Charles Whitfield[87]

Charles Whitfield, MD, identifies both the illness that afflicts many of us and the remedy needed for our healing. Our dis-ease, he claims, has to do with the failure to realize how much of our unhappiness, disappointment, and frustration with life is the result of "looking elsewhere." When we feel empty, confused, lost, and the like, we instinctively search for relief in someone, something, somewhere, that will somehow dispel the darkness that at times hovers cloud-like over our minds and hearts. Surely, we think and feel, there is a fix for my dilemma "elsewhere."

Whitfield redirects our longing for relief where it needs to go, within rather than outside of ourselves. Stop searching outside, he counsels, and instead *abide inside*. Stop expecting to be fulfilled by another person or a different set of circumstances. Rather, rest in the wisdom, depth, and beauty that is you.

Scottish theologian William Barclay said there are two important days in our lives – the day we are born, and the day we discover why. The "why" according to Whitfield is to "know ourselves in a deeper, richer, and more profound way." His prescription for our addiction to looking "elsewhere" and the way to its healing consists of being "truly in relationship with our selves, with others, and with the God of our understanding." This requires spending quiet time acknowledging and accepting our thoughts and feelings, spending quality time sharing honestly with those who matter most to us, and spending prayerful time wherein we surrender to the Mystery in whose embrace we "live and move and have our being" (Acts 17:28).

When we resist the temptation to look "elsewhere," when we realize a sense of inner completeness, and when we come to know and value who we are, we become able to see clearly, connect deeply, and find our way through the maze of conflicting relationships, responsibilities, and possibilities that is life.

A PATH WITH HEART

You ask whether your verses are any good. You ask me. You have asked others before this. You send them to magazines. You compare them with other poems ... I beg you to stop doing that sort of thing. You are looking outside, and that is what you should most avoid right now ... There is only one thing you should do. Go into yourself ... confess to yourself whether you would have to die if you were forbidden to write ... ask yourself in the most silent hour of your night: must I write. Dig into yourself for a deep answer. And if the answer rings out in assent, if you meet this solemn question with a strong, simple "I must," then build your life in accordance with this necessity ...
— Rainer Maria Rilke[88]

In the passage above, German poet Rainer Maria Rilke is responding to an aspiring poet's query regarding the quality of his work. "Am I a good poet?" "Do I have what it takes to succeed?" "How does my writing compare to yours and to others?" Rilke disparages such questions and points the young man in the only direction in which he will find the reassurance he is seeking – within.

Rilke urges the young poet to "confess to yourself whether you would have to die if you were forbidden to write." Not many of us would feel we have to die if we are not able to follow our dreams, but there is a kind of death we may experience if we are not true to ourselves – the kind that makes it difficult to look in the mirror. What is it I must choose if I am to live with integrity, is a question that can arise in both our personal and professional lives. Should I speak up or keep quiet? Should I act now or remain patient? Should I hold tightly to my beliefs or loosen my grip? What must I do or not do, say or not say, in order to be aligned with my deepest truth and values?

Rilke's advice is good counsel not only regarding major life directions but when it comes to making daily decisions as well. He encourages us to go inside, to connect with our heart, and to discover there what gives us a sense of peace and passion. His counsel is consistent with that of author and spiritual teacher Carlos Castaneda who writes, "Look at every path closely and deliberately. Try it as many times as you think is necessary, then ask yourself, and yourself alone … Does this path have a heart?"[89]

AVOIDING THE VOID

When the people saw that Moses delayed to come down from the mountain, the people gathered around Aaron and said to him, "Come, make gods for us, who shall go before us; as for this Moses, the man who brought us up out of the land of Egypt, we do not know what has happened to him."
– Exodus 32:1

The addictions that afflict many of us as we meander through life are false gods that we worship in order to fill an inner void, an emptiness that, if we embraced it, could make way for the Presence for which we long. A subtle example of a void-filling false god is the busyness with which many of us occupy ourselves so as not to be alone with our thoughts and feelings. People in our culture will do almost anything to avoid the void of being still, silent, and alone. We seek meaning and a sense of purpose through relationships and productivity, both of which are good, but we often fail to experience the value of ourselves independent of people and supercharged activity.

When I originally wrote that paragraph for my book *Finding God Beyond Religion*, I put it in the context of the story of the Israelite's worship of a golden calf as they awaited Moses' return from his rendezvous with Yahweh (Exodus 32:1-6). In the desert without a leader, the people grew restless and impatient. They didn't trust themselves to the difficulties of their journey, so they settled for what made them feel good momentarily, an idol that filled the void created by their fears and insecurities.

It may not be obvious why worshipping an idol could be considered an addiction, for we usually equate addictive behaviour with some form of substance or conduct abuse – drugs, alcohol, and gambling are obvious examples. But from the Latin *addicere*, to be addicted means to sell out, to abandon, or betray. It is in other words a turning away from what is of value, a choice to satisfy a deep need or longing with something superficial.

Almost any activity can be addictive. Watching television, shopping, eating, and working can become a form of selling out, a way to avoid the emptiness we may experience when life feels like a desert of doubt and uncertainty. Although these can be good and even necessary activities, when we enter into them as an escape from life's difficulties, they become "false gods" that serve to temporarily satisfy a greater need, that of connecting with our deeper, sacred self.

It is tempting to get busy when there is nothing to do and to find something or someone to occupy the time when time hangs heavy. But a better way might be to first take a deep breath and then walk into the void, for we might just discover that "the Presence for which we long" awaits us in the stillness, silence, and emptiness within.

BEAUTIFULLY FRAGILE

We are all just a car crash,
a diagnosis,
an unexpected phone call,
a newfound love
or a broken heart away
from becoming a
completely
different
person.
How beautifully fragile are
we that so many things can
take but a moment
to alter
who
we are
for forever.
– Samuel Decker Thompson[90]

We don't like to think about it, but deep down we know that any number of things can happen to us or to those we love – things that can bring us to our knees and life as we know it to a screeching halt. It is usually something painful that does this, but even "a newfound love" can lead to a diffi-cult undoing of the person we've known our self to be.

Poet and author Samuel Decker Thompson refers to us – our vulnerability to life's unpredictable and unwanted occurrences – as being "beautifully fragile." This is not an easy-on-the-eye-or-heart beauty, for it doesn't feel very beautiful when our life is upended. It isn't very appealing to live on the tender edge of anguish. It's anything but attractive to know we are a breath away from a broken heart. But if we step back from the fear of being wounded by unexpected events, we may sense that it is only because we love that we are capable of being hurt. It is usually through pain that we are beckoned to become "a completely different person," one who is compassionate, who values living in the moment, and who realizes that the true priority in life is our relationships with one another.

Another element of fragility's veiled and paradoxical beauty has to do with the fact that it is a thread connecting us to each other, no matter what our differences – rich and poor, believer and atheist, Caucasian and colourful. We are all adrift in the same boat. We are all susceptible to the heartache that accompanies loss. We are all powerless to prevent the harsh realities that can and do touch our lives and those we care about. We are all a mere moment away from being altered forever. There is a beauty even in the most difficult truths, and the truth is that we are fragile together.

CROSSING A THRESHOLD

To acknowledge and cross a new threshold is always a challenge. It demands courage and also a sense of trust in whatever is emerging. This becomes essential when a threshold opens suddenly in front of you, one for which you had no preparation. This could be illness, suffering, or loss. Because we are so engaged with the world, we usually forget how fragile life can be and how vulnerable we always are. It takes only a couple of seconds for a life to change irreversibly. Suddenly you stand on

*completely strange ground and a new course of life has to be
embraced.*

– John O'Donohue[91]

A threshold is an entrance to something significant, something new, something challenging, and often something mysterious. In one sense, we are always standing at a threshold, always on the cusp of the unknown, for at any time our life could change in ways we never imagined – for better or for worse.

John O'Donohue references the worse when he states that crossing a threshold could mean having to face harsh realities such as "illness, suffering, or loss." Certainly, these and other misfortunes call us to enter and embrace new territory both within and without, challenging us to develop coping skills we didn't know we had.

But the fragility and vulnerability O'Donohue speaks of does not exist just in relation to the stark and random nature of life, the fact that something hurtful can happen to anyone at any time, but to our susceptibility to the sacred. Whether we know it or not – and usually we do not – there is an underlying hallowedness to life. This may be easier to sense in "magical moments" of beauty, joy, and peace, but even when life is difficult or merely uneventful, there lurks a spiritual presence beneath the surface of the ordinary. Psychologist James Finley refers to this as the "transcendent dimension of the concrete immediacy of the present moment."[92] In other words, everything and everyone is both down-to-earth and out-of-this-world at the same time. It is possible to wake up to the felt sense of this life-altering truth anytime, anywhere.

Although we may have tread upon it often, we "stand on completely strange ground" when we realize that everyday tasks, common places, and familiar faces, are a threshold to what is ultimate and infinite. At home, at work, or wherever we are, there is a spiritual presence to engage and "a new course of life" to be embraced.

DISCOVERING OUR SACRED SELF

Be the ... Lewis and Clark of your own streams and oceans; explore your own higher latitudes ... be a Columbus to whole new worlds within you, opening new channels, not of trade, but of thought ... it is easier to sail many thousand miles through cold and storm and cannibals ... than it is to explore the private sea; the Atlantic and Pacific Ocean of one's being ...
– Fenton Johnson[93]

Living as we do in the 21st century, there doesn't seem to be much left to discover on planet earth – no oceans, islands, or continents have eluded our searching gaze. This being the case, our explorations are now focused on space – that seemingly infinite cosmos that calls for a daring and adventurous spirit. At the same time, author Fenton Johnson offers another realm of fascination for the courageous among us, one that is so close at hand that we easily overlook it – the uncharted terrain of the soul.

The reason it is "easier to sail many thousand miles through cold and storm and cannibals" than to examine our soul is because soul searching requires the disciplines of silence and solitude, which enable us to hear the voiceless voice and sense the precious presence that lies within. Silence and solitude can be daunting not only because many of us are addicted to noise and busyness, but because being quietly alone puts us face-to-face with aspects of ourselves that are less than attractive – pettiness, fear, insecurity, vindictiveness, negativity, and the like. These dark shouters can cause us to stop short in our exploration, for they have the power to convince us that there is nothing more to be found, that we are what is wrong with us.

One who did not allow his journey of self-discovery to be diverted by those sinister voices was monk and mystic Thomas Merton. Knowing that we are all more than our imperfections, Merton wrote, "*No matter how low you may have fallen in your own esteem, bear in mind that if you delve deeply into yourself, you will discover holiness there.*"[94] The holiness Merton refers to is not that of piety, purity, and perfection, but a simple sacredness that is our essence no matter how flawed we may be.

It is the task of each one of us to venture into the unknown within, where we can discover our own "higher latitudes," the holiness at the centre of ourselves.

HEEDING THE VOICELESS VOICE

When the book and the bird disagree, always believe the bird.
    – John James Audubon

As I wrote in my previous book *In Sync with the Sacred, Out of Step with the World*, authenticity is first and foremost a matter of being attuned and responsive to the sacred within – to an instinct, an intuition, a sixth sense, a deep voiceless voice that can be "heard" even in a crowd. This inner guide may at times call us to live apart from others, but it surely summons us to follow a road less travelled; that is, it calls us to turn away from the conventional wisdom of society, those ways of thinking, believing, and behaving that go unquestioned – busy is *good*, more is better, success equals wealth ...

Authenticity often requires the courage to be different,

to stand out, to be considered odd, and perhaps even a threat by those who find their identity and security in the *status quo*. This kind of authenticity challenges us to heed the promptings of an inner wisdom whose "voiceless voice" guides us to our Truth – that is, to the recognition of how we must live if we are to experience the likes of meaning, peace, joy, and satisfaction.

None of us are immune to the ethos that surrounds us; we are all impacted by the messages that come from our families, friends, faith communities, and society in general. The "sound" of their influence can make it difficult to hear and to trust an intuitive voice, one that may be calling us to take a "road less travelled." Being busy may be good, but so is being quiet and reflective. More might in some cases be better, but sometimes the simplicity of having less is more. Success is most often equated with the accumulation of wealth, but doing what is meaningful may lead to a richness that money can never buy.

Every spiritual tradition encourages adherents to follow the dictates of an inner wisdom; they all invite us to live in contradiction (against the word) to the culture of conformity. That culture with its emphasis on affluence, appearance, and accomplishment, is not necessarily flawed, but because we are spiritual beings its material focus can never satisfy our deepest longings.

It is nothing short of prophetic to be true to the Truth within, for doing so puts us at odds with most others. But by heeding the "voiceless voice" we find ourselves in the good company of people like bird biographer John James Audubon who opined that, when the bird (inner wisdom) and the book (conventional wisdom) disagree, always believe the bird!

HOMELESS NO MORE

The human drama of homelessness takes many forms, wears many faces; psychological disturbances in which we are no longer at home in the intimacy of our own lived experience; a troubled marriage in which no dwelling can be found in a relationship we assumed would always prevail; a crisis of faith in which our religious tradition since childhood ceases to be what we deep down have come to believe, or at least its truths are no longer true for us in the way they used to be ... a series of illnesses in which our body is no longer the home we have known it to be; the final, inevitable homelessness of death. It is a homelessness so boundless that the never questioned assurance of tomorrow's sunrise no longer shelters us.

– James Finley[95]

You may not be reading these words at home, but it's a pretty safe bet that you have one. Unlike a growing number of people, most of us have the comfort and security of a place to live – a place to eat, sleep, relax, interact with family and friends, and shelter from the cold or heat. But what psychologist James Finley points out is that homelessness has to do with more than the absence of a physical place from which we come and go. Our minds and marriages, our beliefs and bodies, and ultimately life itself can all be "places" that offer the warmth of home – until they don't.

Everything we have and are is impermanent. Everyone we know and love is in our life temporarily, as we are in theirs. We grow accustomed to each other, to the life we have created for ourselves, and to the "assurance of tomorrow's sunrise," but homelessness in its many forms is never far away. This realization need not be sombre, but it is sober. The awareness that we will lose all we have can shake us up and wake us from a semi-sleep that takes life and relationships for granted; it can redirect our minds and hearts to the home that is our soul.

In the deepest spiritual sense, home is not where we reside but where we choose to *abide*; it is not a dwelling place but the sacred inner space where we are in union with the divine. When we "hang out" there, when we stop to rest and refresh ourselves in the home that is our soul, the comings and goings that exist in our life in the world become more reverent and real, more passionate and compassionate.

Although we may not presently experience any of the faces that homelessness wears, we will surely encounter it at some point(s) on life's journey. If we discover and take shelter in the peaceful stillness of our soul, even the homelessness of death may not feel so ominous.

IT'S HARD ON THE SOUL

Only yesterday our vet told us that our sweet Golden Retriever is very ill, and tonight we're supposed to go out to dinner with some friends. I'm torn, because we've been scheduling, canceling, and rescheduling this dinner for six months, and part of me really wants to go. But part of me is dealing with the loss of the family dog. What I'm aware of in this moment is how often I need to put my soul aside in order to carry on with the demands of life. We all do. Life goes on, despite our personal struggles. You lose your father on a Wednesday; corporate America expects you back at the office Monday. It's hard on the soul.

– John Eldredge[96]

First of all, for those readers who have never had a pet that is part of their family, know that the death of a family pet is a very real and great loss; like the loss of a person, it can be very hard, very sad, and as in the case with someone we love, a pet's death requires grieving.

John Eldredge uses the dilemma occasioned by the imminent death of his dog to make the point that some things touch us so deeply they require our whole-hearted physical, emotional, and spiritual presence. At the same time, responsibilities, demands, and requirements of a personal and professional nature can make it difficult to honour matters of the heart and soul.

How are we to manage such unmanageable situations? How are we to negotiate what seems impossible? How can we be true to who we are and still show up at the office on Monday? There is no hard and fast answer to questions of this nature, for they are not to be answered as much as they are to be lived. Every situation that presents us with this type of dilemma is an invitation to recognize the reality of our deepest self. Because life is full of practicalities, it's easy to function only on that level. But when we realize the importance of our soul, we can at least begin to take it into consideration when we encounter conflicting demands.

The title of Eldredge's book is *Get Your Life Back*. Many of us have given the lion's share of our life – our time and energy – to external realities, but have not honoured our whole self. Perhaps it's time to take our life back, lest we regret not having done so until it's too late.

LIFE WITHIN LIFE

Where do we go when we sleep? A third of our life is lived underground, and deep down inside us a stream will rise now and then to the surface, trailing visions into our waking. Yet what if that stream had been watering us all the days of our life and we never knew it? Perhaps there is a life within life, a blessedness that pours through our days and years and we barely suspect it … There is another life … and it is here, just below our skin and our eyelids.

We spend most of our days immersed in the stories we take to be the stuff of our lives. Tale after tale of gain and loss consumes our attention for decades, often a lifetime. And then all of a sudden it is over.

– Roger Housden[97]

Is there a life within life as poet Roger Housden implies? Is there a Self within the self we know ourselves to be? Is there a deeper dimension to our existence that we encounter when we sink beneath consciousness, and that sometimes surfaces in our dreams? It has always struck me as strange that we humans – who pride ourselves for being rational, thinking beings – need to spend so much of our lives asleep. What's with that? Is it just a physical necessity, or might it also have to do with the importance of being in touch with "a blessedness that pours through our days and years"?

It is true that in our conscious state, we are mostly inclined to immerse ourselves in "tale after tale of gain and loss." The practicality of day-to-day existence – our physical, emotional, and relational ups and downs – have the power to consume our attention and prevent us from sensing that a "stream … [has] been watering us all the days of our life." In his song "The River of Dreams," Billy Joel sings about searching for something sacred he has lost. When we lose touch with the "life within life," the presence of the divine at the core of our being, we are disconnected from our sacred source, our true identity, our spiritual essence.

Whether we remember our dreams or not, when we sleep we descend into the stream "just below our skin and eyelids." When we sleep, we become wet with the water of life, we become soaked with the spirit that enlivens not only our body, but our soul; we become "baptized," born again into an awareness of who we truly are, and that life is about more than the "gain and loss that consumes our attention for decades, often a lifetime."

Too often our sleep is restless with worries of the day. Perhaps it would be otherwise if we gave those worries to the God of our understanding – to a Higher or Inner Power however we choose to name it – and gave ourselves permission to dive into the river of dreams, the water of life, the sacred stream that lies beneath the surface of our self.

LOVE AND LAUGH

No one knows what we're doing here. Some have faith that they do, but no one knows.

So we are scared. We are alone. And we end. And we don't know where we go. So we cling to money for comfort. And we chase awards for immortality. And we hide in the routine of our days. But then the night, always the night. Which, when it has you alone, whispers that maybe none of this has any significance. So love everyone you're with because comforting each other on this journey we neither asked for nor understand is the best we can do. And laugh as much as you can.

– Stephan Pastis[98]

The above is pretty serious stuff for a comic strip. "Pearls Before Swine" is the creation of cartoonist Stephan Pastis who in this strip depicts a pig standing on a tree stump wondering out loud about the meaning of existence. It's an uncomfortable truth he is pondering, one we may not spend much time considering as we "hide in the routine of our days."

But we are ultimately alone, and we will end, and we don't really know what lies beyond this life. Disturbing as it can be to contemplate such matters, it's sometimes good to look them in the face, for by doing so we can come to appreciate that life and death are an amazing mystery, as are the people with whom we share them.

Mr. Pig has reached some important conclusions as a result of his ruminations; while we're "on this journey we neither asked for nor understand," it's important to both love and laugh. Mark Twain once said that compassion is language the deaf can hear and the blind can see. Compassion is love in action. Compassion is visceral, it is tangible, and it can bring comfort that is heard by the deaf, seen by the blind, and felt in the hearts of all people. Love truly is "the best we can do."

As for laughter, well, it really is medicine for our souls. In his poem "The Guest House," 13th-century Muslim mystic Rumi counsels us to meet unwelcomed guests at the door of our hearts, laughing – even if they're a crowd of sorrows. This is surely a tall task but one worth striving for, because laughter builds an immune system that robs sorrow of its power to sour – that is, to infect us with the likes of hopelessness, fear, and cynicism.

"But then the night, always the night." This, for many of us, is the time when we are most vulnerable to fearful thoughts and feelings. When instead of "clinging to money for comfort," or choosing to "chase awards for immortality," we face our fears, then the night becomes like day and we may find ourselves both loving and laughing more easily and more often – even when it's dark.

PESSIMISM / OPTIMISM

When asked if I am pessimistic or optimistic about the future, my answer is always the same: If you look at the science about what is happening on earth and aren't pessimistic, you don't understand data. But if you meet the people who are working to restore this earth and the lives of the poor, and you aren't optimistic, you haven't got a pulse. What I see everywhere in the world are ordinary people willing to confront despair, power, and incalculable odds in order to restore some semblance of grace, justice, and beauty in the world.

— Paul Hawken[99]

It has been said jokingly that pessimists are people who spend too much time around optimists! Some positive-thinking people have a Pollyanna-like attitude that renders them unwilling or unable to be realistic. For these annoying optimists, the proverbial glass is always half-full even when it's not.

Paul Hawken, author and environmental activist, knows there is reason for both pessimism and optimism when it comes to our life on planet earth. He encourages us to not let the overwhelming nature of dire circumstances – poverty, pandemics, global warming, racism, war … – blind us to the good happening everywhere, every day. It is important to acknowledge harsh realities, but even more important to recognize and celebrate the ever-present goodness at the heart of life.

Falling prey to pessimism is a possibility not only with regard to global and societal conditions, but also in realms closer to home. We can be overwhelmed by troubles of a personal nature. We can, for instance, lose heart when confronted by chronic illness, loss of a loved one, a financial crisis, addiction afflicting our self or someone close to us, a troubled marriage, or friction with a co-worker or boss. Any number of situations and relationships can seem beyond repair and cause us to lose hope.

But here, too, there is room for optimism. Hawken is buoyed by ordinary people willing to confront incalculable odds. In order to overcome personal difficulties, we need to step up, we must be the "ordinary people" who by refusing to succumb to the gravitational pull of pessimism can remain hopeful and engaged in the midst of trying circumstances.

The ability to overcome adversity is not a matter of willpower or the "power of positive thinking." Rather, what enables us to prevail is a radical openness to our soul, the spiritual force at the core of our being that makes it possible to work tirelessly to bring "some semblance of grace, justice, and beauty" to our corner of the world.

QUERENCIA

In bullfighting there is a place in the ring where the bull feels safe. If he can reach this place, he stops running and can gather his full strength. He is no longer afraid … It is the job of the matador to know where this sanctuary lies, to be sure the bull does not have time to occupy his place of wholeness. This safe place for the bull is called the querencia. For humans, the querencia is the safe place in our inner world. When a person finds their querencia in full view of the matador, they are calm and peaceful …

— Rachel Remen[100]

There are times in all of our lives when we are like the bull in a bullfight – times when we feel attacked, wounded, vulnerable, and scared. The loss of a loved one, serious health concerns, being let go from a job, the breakup of a relationship, and other trials and traumas can rock us to the core. In reaction to life's challenges, we may, like an injured bull, go on the attack. Inside, however, it is fear that grips our heart. No one wants to be afraid, but it is only when we face what hurts us and when we feel the feelings resulting from our wounds that we can experience the inner calm and peace that enables us to return to the "fight" with renewed vigour.

For author and physician Rachel Remen, the bullfight has involved a lifelong battle with Crohn's disease. Dr. Remen discovered that by retreating to her *querencia* (soul), she found the ability to face and embrace the reality of her incurable situation. Like hers, our life's difficulties are an invitation to find our *querencia* and to experience the safety, calm, and wholeness that can only be found within. It is there, in our deepest self, that we know we are more than what is happening to us, and it is from there that we can look life in the eye without fear – or at least without being paralyzed by it.

But it is as if the matador (life) is trying to prevent us from discovering our "safe place." Its many demands and responsibilities, its allurements and drama, and its message to soldier on, can keep us from stopping, resting, and regaining our "full strength." It can be courageous to heed the invitation to stop and to rest because doing so can appear to be weak. But if we see that our afflictions are a dark gift, a blessing in disguise, they can be embraced as the way to gather our full strength, and thus become our best self.

RESTING IN OUR SOUL

*When we understand, we are at the center of the circle,
and all the while "yes" and "no" chase one another
around the circumference.*
– Chuang Tzu[101]

*We dance 'round in a ring and suppose.
But the secret sits in the middle and knows.*
– Robert Frost[102]

Chuang Tzu, a Chinese philosopher who lived in the third century BCE, and Robert Frost a 20th-century American poet, both speak of what appears to be a timeless reality, namely, that we are often alienated from the core of our being, the essence of who we are, our spiritual home base. While we are running around in circles trying to find our way in life, there is a place of understanding beneath the "yes" and "no" of likes and dislikes, opinions and attitudes, questions and conclusions that preoccupy us most of our waking hours. While we "suppose," propose, and impose, there is an inner wisdom, a "secret" that knows what our minds do not.

When we are out of touch with this sacred dimension of ourselves, we forget that we are more than what we do and more than what happens to us; we tend be off balance, thrown by life's ups and downs, its trials and triumphs. We easily lose our deeper sense of self to the forces of victory and defeat, success and failure. We become reactive rather than responsive when life is stressful, critical of ourselves rather than compassionate when we don't achieve our goals, judgmental of others rather than accepting when they don't meet our needs and expectations.

It is a daily decision and discipline to go from the surface to the centre of ourselves, from dancing "'round in a ring" to resting in our soul. But how might this movement be accomplished? Psalm 46:10 from the Hebrew scriptures invites us to "Be still, and know that I am God." Whatever our notion of the divine may be, our best chance to connect with it and with our deepest self comes when we are still and silent. It is nothing less than radical to opt for even a few moments of stillness and silence in our "crazy busy" world but being connected with our "centre" and attuned to the "secret" within, is essential for our physical, mental, emotional, and spiritual well-being.

Difficult as it may be, if we make living in a more reflective manner a priority, we will be better for it, and so will those with whom we live and work.

SEEKING SANCTUARY

When I was a kid, "sanctuary" meant only one thing. It was the big room with the stained glass windows and hard wooden benches where my family worshipped every Sunday …

Today, "sanctuary" is as vital as breathing to me. Sometimes I find it in churches, monasteries, and other sites formally designated "sacred." But more often I find it in places sacred to my soul: in the natural world, in the company of a faithful friend, in solitary or shared silence, in the ambience of a good poem or good music.

Sanctuary is wherever I find safe space to regain my bearings, reclaim my soul, heal my wounds, and return to the world as a wounded healer.

— Parker Palmer[103]

According to author and educator Parker Palmer, a healing and empowering sense of sanctuary can be found not only in religious experiences, but also in so-called "secular" experiences, not only apart from the world, but in the midst of it. Sanctuary exists wherever and with whomever we can let down our guard, be our selves, and open our hearts to the mystery of life.

The renewal we all need as a result of the stressful responsibilities of our personal and professional lives is often overlooked. We push ourselves to accomplish one more task, meet one more deadline, and attend to one more person's need, before we give ourselves permission to rest – which often means falling into our chair or bed exhausted. Many of us were taught that self-care is selfish, but although there are times when the demands of work and relationships must come first, if we continually ignore our physical, mental, emotional, and spiritual needs, not only we, but those around us will pay the price.

Physician and humanitarian Albert Schweitzer once said, "The only ones among you who will be really happy are those who will have sought and found how to serve." Sanctuary is about self-care for our own sake and that of others; it is a womb-like experience from which we can be birthed into the world. Finding and resting in sanctuary is important not only because we are important, but because without the renewal it offers, we will not be at our best to serve each other.

SELF-CARE FIRST

Compassion, like charity, begins at home. The first step toward deep healing is self-healing. Only after we have remembered to respect and care for ourselves can we truly enter into "kinship with all beings." If we try to help others before we have healed our wounds and developed compassion for ourselves, we may

find that the basis of our rescuing and helping of others is
codependency rather than co-creation.

— Joan Borysenko[104]

When I first read psychologist Joan Borysenko's *Fire in the Soul*, the following came to mind: "Should there be a loss of cabin pressure, oxygen masks will automatically drop from the compartment above your seat. Please adjust your own mask before assisting a child or another passenger." Most readers will recognize this as an instruction given by flight attendants prior to takeoff; their announcement is a reminder of the truth that caring for ourselves best positions us to care for others.

Given the conventional message many of us have internalized from family, faith communities, and society in general, taking care of ourselves first can feel counterintuitive; it can feel self-serving, and even selfish. We are to care for others first, those voices say, and for ourselves only after everyone else's needs are met. But compassion does indeed begin at the home that is our self. "Adjusting our own mask" first is good counsel in the physical realm, for without proper nutrition, exercise, and rest we would eventually be unable to perform the simplest tasks that might prove helpful to others.

Self-care is also essential in the more subtle arena of the soul. Here the question becomes what do we need to do, or cease doing, in order to be in touch with our deepest self, for it is only from this place of inner connection that we can be our best for others. Perhaps we need to spend some alone time now and then, or to immerse ourselves in nature, relax with family and friends, or pray/meditate. Or maybe we need to drink less alcohol, work less, spend less time in front of the television, or on social media, for these activities often result in our becoming a stranger to our selves.

Yes, there are times and circumstances in which it is necessary to set aside our own needs and preferences in order to appropriately attend to another; this is especially true in times of crisis or when danger lurks. But in the long run of our relationships, it is essential to "respect and care for ourselves" physically and spiritually, for we can always count on a loss of "cabin pressure" from time to time.

SPOT OF GRACE

Each person is born with an unencumbered spot, free of expectation and regret, free of ambition and embarrassment, free of fear and worry, an umbilical spot of grace where we were each first touched by God. It is this spot of grace that issues peace. Psychologists call this spot the Psyche, theologians call it the Soul …

To know this spot of inwardness is to know who we are, not by surface markers of identity, not by where we work or what we wear or how we like to be addressed but by feeling our place in relation to the Infinite and by inhabiting it.

— Mark Nepo[105]

The Greek word for soul and butterfly is the same – *psyche*. This verbal anomaly suggests that our soul, the "spot of grace where we were first touched by God," is a dimension of ourselves that matures gradually. Like the caterpillar that through metamorphosis is transformed into the butterfly it is capable of being, we evolve into our best self. It takes time and it takes the experience of loves and losses, the humiliation of failure, and the humbling grace of success to teach us that we are more than the "surface markers of identity."

What if we were to live from this deep place of psyche

or soul? Well, we might possess a quiet calm even though our life is filled with the chaos of conflicted relationships and deadlines too close to meet. We might also find ourselves awash in an unexplainable deep joy despite the existence of painful losses. We might be taken hold by a firmness and resolve as we voice an opinion that is unpopular even though it is hard to be the odd person out. And we might find ourselves nonplussed in the face of a derogatory comment that would wound the most callous among us.

When we inhabit our soul, we live in *response* not in *reaction* to the events and relationships that make up our life. When we are in touch with our "spot of grace," we find our identity *within* and know that we are more than what we do or what happens to us. When we know "our place in relation to the Infinite," we experience the freedom poet Mark Nepo writes about – freedom from expectation and regret, ambition and embarrassment, fear and worry.

Determination, patience, and the willingness to open ourselves to the transforming forces of life are the cocoon that enables us to become a human butterfly – the person of delicate and enduring beauty we are meant to be.

THAT I MAY SEE

The purpose of "looking" is to survive, to cope, to manipulate, to discern what is useful, agreeable, or threatening to the Me, what enhances or diminishes the Me ... When, on the other hand, I SEE – suddenly I am all eyes, I forget this Me, am liberated from it.

– Frederick Franck[106]

Artist and author Frederick Franck makes an important distinction between looking and seeing. The former is a function of the ego (Me), while the latter is a matter of the soul. It is important to look, because doing so enables us to maneuver through the day, to assess the significance of people and situations, and to then determine whether or how to relate to them. Looking is basic, it is a survival mechanism that keeps us from bumping into what may be harmful and helps us decide what can be useful. But *seeing* takes things to a different and deeper level.

In his poem "Auguries of Innocence," William Blake writes, "We are led to believe a lie when we see with not thro [*sic*] the eye."[107] The lie Blake refers to is not a falsehood but incompleteness; we are more than meets the eye. The lie is to believe that we are only physical, mental, emotional beings who are separate from one another and whose lives will end when our bodies die. But when seen "thro the eye" we catch a glimpse of the eternal truth that everything and everyone is united by a common spiritual bond – there is an undying sacredness that permeates our being and our planet.

It is important to have a healthy ego, but an undue or primary focus on the ego limits us. When I look at everything and everyone only for how they can enhance or diminish Me, I am likely to overlook, undervalue, and possibly mistreat them. Looking in this sense is a form of blindness to the larger truth of the dignity and relatedness of humanity, and the sanctity of the earth that sustains us all.

Our physical eyes enable us to look at our surroundings, but the "eyes of faith," the conviction that there is more to behold, make it possible to see beneath appearances. Because most of us are prone to looking without seeing, it might be helpful, whether we consider ourselves religious or not, to start every day with the statement uttered by the blind man who approached Jesus for healing: "Lord, let me see again" (Luke 18:41).

THE GIFT OF LONELINESS

What then can we do with our essential aloneness which so often breaks into our consciousness as the experience of a desperate sense of loneliness: ... Instead of running away from our loneliness ... we have to protect it and turn it into a fruitful solitude ... the movement from loneliness to solitude ... is the beginning of any spiritual life because it is the movement from the restless senses to the restful spirit, from the outward-reaching cravings to the inward-reaching search ...

— Henri Nouwen[108]

The experience of feeling lonely is a catalyst for much of our addictive behaviour. This inner ache, this sense of emptiness, can fuel unhealthy cravings for alcohol and drugs, for overwork and binge eating, for compulsive shopping, obsessive use of email, phones, television, video games, and all the many ways we try to fill the void. We will do almost anything to escape feeling lonely.

Dutch priest and psychologist Henri Nouwen makes an important distinction between loneliness and solitude. The latter is a state of wholeness that lies beneath our ill-at-easeness. When we attempt to run from feeling lonely, we miss out on the interior sense of peace and contentment without which "restless senses" and "outward-reaching" can rule and ruin our lives.

When we allow noise and activity to fill us, there is no room for the "restful spirit," the inner repose and sense of companionship that enabled Henry David Thoreau to write from his cabin on Walden Pond, "I have a great deal of company in my house; especially in the morning when nobody calls."[109] In a similar vein, an anonymous author has written, "Never less alone than when alone."

Theologian Paul Tillich wrote, "Loneliness expresses the pain of being alone, solitude expresses the glory of being alone."[110] Whether we are by ourselves or in the company of others, loneliness can be a gift if we choose to linger with rather than run from it, for loneliness is not a matter of being disconnected from others. Rather, it is being disconnected from our deep, soul-self. If we resist the impulse to busy ourselves and instead befriend our "essential aloneness," we might find that we are not so alone after all and that we are able to relate to others without being needy or dependent.

TOUCHING A SOUL

Your accomplishments are not the most important parts of your life. Besides, any record you break will sooner or later be broken by someone else. Whether you excel in sports or in work, there will always be someone who comes along after you and does what you did but even better. The bar for success will only keep rising. It's satisfying to strive for something greater, but keep in mind that none of us will have really succeeded unless we've done something to touch another human being's soul.

— Eliot Marshall[111]

It can be a pretty empty feeling to come to the end of a day and find yourself saying, "I didn't accomplish a thing." When we haven't begun, made progress on, or completed any project, task, or endeavour, it is likely that we will feel we've wasted our time, or perhaps even that we're wasting our life. It may in fact be true that we could or should have gotten something done, but what is not true is that accomplishments are the measure of our worth; they are not the gold standard that determines our significance as a person.

Eliot Marshall spent a lifetime trying and failing to win acceptance through accomplishments. When he woke up to the futility of his efforts, Marshall realized that the recognition and acclaim that often follows from accomplishing our goals can feed and fatten our ego, but no amount of accomplishments will ever satisfy our deepest longings. We can find ourselves careening like bumper cars from one endeavour to another, one person to another, one task, project, one venture to another in an attempt to satisfy a longing that can only be fulfilled by touching another human soul.

Soul is a word that refers to the sacred depth of our self. Soul is a dimension of our being wherein we experience meaning, connection, passion, and compassion. We are most alive when we are one with our soul. Touching a soul involves relating to a person in a way that makes them aware of their sacredness and makes them feel more alive. It is not usually extraordinary or dramatic encounters that make people aware of their spiritual core, rather, it is the quality of our presence, our full focus on them that communicates the truth that they are worthwhile, valuable, a one-of-a-kind, sacred self. Days may go by during which we don't accomplish much, but if we are able to introduce just one person to their soul, we can count ourselves successful at what matters most.

NOTES

1. André Breton, *Mad Love*, rev. ed. (Lincoln, NB: Bison Books, 1988).

2. Newton Minow, "Under the Law," Azquotes.com/author/21335-newton_n_minow

3. John Monczunski, *Facebook post*, September 9, 2020.

4. James Broughton, "Curve Your Straight," in *Little Sermons of the Big Joy* (Philadelphia: Insight to Riot Press, 1994), 4.

5. Julia Cameron, *Prayers from a Nonbeliever* (New York: Jeremy P. Tarcher, 2003,) 7.

6. C. S. Lewis, *The Four Loves* (SanFrancisco: HarperOne, 2017), 155.

7. Billy Collins, "Aimless Love," in *Aimless Love: New and Selected Poems* (New York: Random House, 2013), 9–10.

8. Joshua Becker, https://www.becomingminimalist. com/on-living-countercultural-lives/

9. Jack Kornfield, *After the Ecstasy, the Laundry* (New York: Bantam Books, 2001), 239.

10. Richard Carlson, *Don't Sweat the Small Stuff and It's All Small Stuff* (New York: MJF Books, 1997), 229.

11. Anna Quindlen, *A Short Guide to a Happy Life* (New York: Random House, 2000), 25–26.

12. Etty Hillesum, *An Interrupted Life* (New York: Washington Square Press, 1985), 229.

13. Charlotte Joko Beck, azquotes.com/author/1111-Joko_Beck

14. Graham Turner, *The Power of Silence* (NY: Bloomsbury, 2012), 81.

15. Thomas Merton, *Love and Living* (New York: Houghton Mifflin Harcourt, 1965), 11.

16. James Hollis, *What Matters Most* (New York: Gotham Books, 2009), 147.

17. Broughton, "Take the Whole Kit" in *Little Sermons*, 7.

18. Peter Viereck, *Source Book of Wit & Wisdom* (Canton: Communication Resources, 1996), 29.

19. Thomas Moore, *Meditations on the Monk Who Dwells in Daily Life* (New York: HarperCollins Publishers, 1994), 1.

20. Rachel Remen, *Kitchen Table Wisdom* (New York: Riverhead Books, 2006), 75.

21. Diana Butler-Bass, *Grounded: Finding God in the World* (San Francisco: HarperOne, 2015), 242.

22. Surya Das, *Awakening the Buddhist Heart* (New York: Broadway Books, 2000), 24–25.

23. George Carlin, https://quotepark.com/quotes/1771548-george-carlin-i-want-to-live-my-next-life-backwards-you-start-o/

24. Anne Lamott, *Traveling Mercies: Some Thoughts on Faith* (New York: Anchor Books, 1999), 126.

25. Roger Housden, *Dropping the Struggle* (Novato: New World Library, 2016), 8.

26. Belden Lane, *Backpacking with the Saints* (New York: Oxford University Press, 2015), 135.

27. Anne Lamott, *Traveling Mercies*, 143.

28. Robert Coles, *Dorothy Day: A Radical Devotion* (Reading: Addison-Wesley Company, Inc., 1987), xviii.

29. Das, *Awakening the Buddhist Heart*, 170–71.

30. Thomas Moore, *The Re-Enchantment of Everyday Life* (New York: HarperCollins Publishers, 1996), 87–88.

31. David Rakoff, *Half Empty* (New York: Doubleday, 2010), 89.

32. Anne Lamott, *Hallelujah Anyway: Rediscovering Mercy* (New York: Riverhead Books, 2017), 8–9.

33. Karen Miller, "Mistakes and Forgiveness," *The Sun Magazine*, February 2021, 33.

34. Roger Housden, *Keeping the Faith Without a Religion* (Boulder: Sounds True, 2014), 49.

35. Robert Frost, "The Secret Sits" in *The Poetry of Robert Frost*, ed. Edward Connery Lathem (New York: Henry Holt and Company, Inc., 1979), 362.

36. Ernest Kurtz, and Katherine Ketcham, *The Spirituality of Imperfection* (New York: Bantam Books, 1992), 42.

37. Parker Palmer, *Let Your Life Speak: Listening for the Voice of Vocation* (San Francisco: Jossey-Bass, 2000), 7.

38. James Finley, "Merton's Path to the Palace of Nowhere," audio series (Boulder, CO: Sounds True, 2004).

39. Veronique Vienne, *The Art of Imperfection* (New York: Clarkson Potter Publisher, 1999), 10–13.

40. Kurtz and Ketcham, *The Spirituality of Imperfection*, 2–3.

41. James Finley, *The Contemplative Heart* (Notre Dame: Sorin Books, 2000), 29.

42. Mark Nepo, *The One Life We're Given: Finding the Wisdom That Waits in Your Heart* (NY: Atria Books, 2016), 68–69.

43. William Saroyan, as quoted in Kerry Temple, "A Moment's Notice," in *Notre Dame Magazine* Spring (2020), 100.

44. Fritjof Capra, *The Tao of Physics*, 5th ed. (Boston: Shambhala, 2010), 8.

45. Parker Palmer, *On the Brink of Everything: Grace, Gravity, and Getting Old* (Oakland, Berrett-Koehler Publishers, Inc., 2018), 59.

46. Robin Wall Kimmerer, *Braiding Sweetgrass* (Minnesota: Milkweed, 2013), 43.

47. Annie Dillard, *Pilgrim at Tinker Creek* (New York: Harper Perennial, 1974), 13.

48. Broughton, "If You Hanker," in *Little Sermons*, 24.

49. Scott Kelly, *Endurance: A Year in Space, a Lifetime of Discovery* (New York: Alfred A. Knopf, 2017), 360–62.

50. Roger Housden, *Ten Poems to Open Your Heart* (New York: Harmony Books, 2003), 39.

51. H. L. Mencken, *A Mencken Chrestomathy* (1949; rep. New York: Alfred A. Knopf, 1967), 624.

52. Kerry Walters, *Rufus Jones* (Maryknoll: Orbis Books, 2001), 16–17.

53. Shauna Niequist, *Present Over Perfect* (Grand Rapids: Zondervan, 2016), 130.

54. Asher Biemann, *The Martin Buber Reader: Essential Writings* (New York: Palgrave Macmillan, 2002), 193.

55. Teilhard de Chardin, *The Divine Milieu* (New York: Harper&Row Publishers, 1960), 112.

56. Kornfield, *After the Ecstasy, the Laundry*, 290.

57. Amy Jalapeno, https://amyjalapeno.com/2013/03/26/what-chaos-has-to-do-with-bliss-daily-hot-quote/

58. J. Philip Newell, *Christ of the Celts* (San Francisco: Jossey Bass, 2008), 110–11.

59. Mark Nepo, *The Little Book of Awakening* (Newburyport: Plum Island Press, 2000), 111–113.

60. Annie Dillard, *Pilgrim at Tinker Creek*, 143.

61. Daniel Klein, *Every Time I Find the Meaning of Life, They Change It* (New York: Penguin Books, 2015), 10.

62. Annie Dillard, *The Writing Life* (New York: Harper Perennial, 2015), 32.

63. Judith Valente and Charles Reynard, *Twenty Poems to Nourish Your Soul* (Chicago: Loyola Press, 2006), 38–39.

64. Brennan Manning, *The Ragamuffin Gospel* (Colorado Springs: Multnomah Books, 2005), 90–91.

65. Louise Mangan and Nancy Wyse, with Lori Farr, *Living the Christ Life* (Kelowna, BC: Wood Lake Books, 2001), 19.

66. Rumi, in Roger Housden, *Ten Poems to Change Your Life Again and Again* (New York: Harmony Books, 2007), 130.

67. James Finley, *Christian Meditation* (San Francisco: HarperSanFrancisco, 2004), 187.

68. Thomas Merton, *A Man in the Divided Sea* (Norfolk: New Directions, 1946), 88.

69. William Wordsworth, "Intimations of Immortality," in *The Prelude, Selected Poems and Sonnets* (New York: Holt, Rinehart and Winston, 1965), 152, 154.

70. Ed Hayes, "A Seed Psalm," in *Prayers for a Planetary Pilgrim* (Notre Dame: Ave Maria Press, 1988), 109.

71. David Foster Wallace, "Commencement Address Kenyon College," as quoted in David Brooks, *The Second Mountain* (New York: Random House, 2019), 199–200.

72. A. J. Baime, "Do You Believe in Miracles?" in *AARP The Magazine* February/March (2020), 66.

73. Brian McLaren, *The Galapagos Islands* (Minneapolis: Fortress Press, 2019), 183–84.

74. Yogi Berra, with Dave Kaplan, *What Time Is It? You Mean Now?* (New York: Simon & Schuster, 2002), 34, 37.

75. Anthony DeMello, *Taking Flight* (New York: Image Books Doubleday, 1990), 27.

76. Finley, *The Contemplative Heart*, 145.

77. David Rakoff, *Half Empty*, 83.

78. Housden, *Keeping the Faith without a Religion*, 75.

79. Kute Blackson, *You Are the One* (New York: North Star Way, 2016), 169–70.

80. Hunter Thompson, *The Proud Highway: Saga of a Desperate Southern Gentleman, 1955–1967* (New York: Ballantine Books, 1998), https://www.goodreads. com/quotes/47188-life-should-not-be-a-journey-to-the-grave-with

81. Thomas Merton, *Wisdom of the Desert* (New York: New Directions, 1960), 50.

82. Mitch Albom, *Have a Little Faith* (New York: Hyperion, 2009), 6–13.

83. Hafiz, in William Sieghart, *The Poetry Remedy: Prescriptions for the Heart, Mind, and Soul* (New York: Viking Press, 2019), 105.

84. William James, *Varieties of Religious Experience* (New York: The New American Library, 1958), 58.

85. Geneen Marie Haugen, in *Spiritual Ecology*, ed. by Llewellyn Vaughan-Lee (Point Reyes: The Golden Sufi Center, 2013), 165.

86. Wendell Berry, *A Continuous Harmony* (New York: Harcourt Brace Jovanovich, 1972), 6.

87. Charles Whitfield, *Co-Dependence: Healing the Human Condition* (Deerfield Beach: Health Communications, Inc., 1991), 4–5.

88. Rainer Maria Rilke, *Letters to a Young Poet* (New York: The Modern Library, 1984), 5–6.

89. Carlos Castaneda, *Journey to Ixtlan: The Lessons of Don Juan*, in Mark Nepo, *The One Life We're Given*, 101.

90. Samuel Decker Thompson, "Beautifully Fragile," in *Our Fucked Up Hearts* (Underwater Mountains, 2016). https://www.facebook.com/ADudeWritingPoetry/

91. John O'Donohue, *To Bless the Space Between Us* (New York: The Doubleday Broadway Publishing Group, 2008), 49.

92. Finley, *The Contemplative Heart*, 142.

93. Fenton Johnson, *At the Center of All Beauty: Solitude and the Creative Life* (New York: W. W. Norton & Company, 2020), 192.

94. Thomas Merton, in Anne Lamott *Hallelujah Anyway*, 76.

95. Finley, *The Contemplative Heart*, 39–40.

96. John Eldredge, *Get Your Life Back: Everyday Practices for a World Gone Mad* (Nashville: Nelson Books, 2020), 51.

97. Roger Housden, *Ten Poems to Change Your Life* (New York: Harmony Books, 2001), 23.

98. Stephan Pastis, "Pearls Before Swine," *Colorado Springs Gazette*, February 4, 2018.

99. Paul Hawken, in *A Sense of Wonder: The World's Best Writers on the Sacred, the Profane, and the Ordinary*, ed. by Brian Doyle (Maryknoll: Orbis Books, 2016), 189.

100. Rachel Remen, in Jack Kornfield, *No Time Like the Present* (New York: Atria Books, 2017), 69.

101. Stephen Mitchell, *The Enlightened Heart* (New York: HarperPerennial, 1993), xv.

102. Frost, "The Secret Sits," in *The Poetry of Robert Frost*, ed. Lathem, 362.

103. Palmer, *On the Brink of Everything*, 137.

104. Joan Borysenko, *Fire in the Soul: A New Psychology of Spiritual Optimism* (New York: Warner Books, 1993), 194.

105. Mark Nepo, *Unlearning Back to God: Essays on Inwardness* (New York: Khaniqahi Nimatullahi Publications, 2006), 12.

106. Frederick Franck, *The Zen of Seeing* (New York: Vintage Books, 1973), 4–5.

107. William Blake, "Auguries of Innocence," in *The Complete Prose and Poetry of William Blake*, ed. David V. Erdman. (New York: Anchor Books, 1988), 496.

108. Henri Nouwen, *Reaching Out* (New York: Doubleday & Company, Inc, 1975), 22–23.

109. Henry David Thoreau, *Walden* (New York: Alfred A. Knopf, 1992), 89.

110. Paul Tillich, *The Eternal Now* (London: SCM Press, 2003).

111. Eliot Marshall, *The Gospel of Fire: Strategies for Facing Your Fears* (Denver: Lioncrest Publishing, 2019), 43.

ACKNOWLEDGEMENTS

Many thanks to the staff of Old Colorado City's Carnegie Library in Colorado Springs. Much of this book was researched and written in its warm surroundings where I was always made to feel at home. I am grateful as well for my friends Bill Barram, Karen Carney, Charlie Coon, Roger Cormier, Elle Derakhshanian, Joe Price, Patrick McLaughlin, Patrick Smith, and Dale Spencer who have done for me what friends do; offer feedback, support, and encouragement. Along with affirmation, my long-time friend Joan Hosmer provided important research and grammatical recommendations that have made this a better book. I'm indebted to my friend and spiritual guide Jim Finley whose writing inspired several of the reflections that this book comprises and whose influence on my soul has shaped them all. And to Mike Schwartzentruber of Wood Lake Publishing whose editor's eye and writer's heart have helped to shape this book in important ways. Many thanks, Mike.

IN SYNC WITH THE SACRED, OUT OF STEP WITH THE WORLD
EMBRACING AN UNCONVENTIONAL LIFE IN A CULTURE OF CONFORMITY

TOM STELLA

In this richly rewarding book, Tom Stella offers insights into what it means to live a "soul-full" life. More than that, he provides a guide on how to approach life in ways that make soul-sense, even if those ways seem like nonsense to the world around us. Along the way, Stella draws from the wisdom of mystics East and West, as well as from poets, philosophers, and theologians of every persuasion. He, and they, encourage us to live not only out of step with convention, but in sync with the sacred, by whatever name, and by whatever means we discover and follow it.

ISBN 978-1-77343-407-0

5" X 8.5" | 134 PP | PAPERBACK | $19.95

CPR FOR THE SOUL
REVIVING A SENSE OF THE SACRED IN EVERYDAY LIFE

TOM STELLA

"The fact that you are not dead is not sufficient proof that you are alive!" So begins Tom Stella's insightful, important, and inspiring exploration into the life, death, and rebirth of the soul. He shares the deep, eternal wisdom that knows that the lines separating the sacred and the secular, time and eternity, humanity and divinity, are false. Or, at the very least, blurred. God, by whatever name, is found in the midst of everyday life, work, and relationships. All people, all creation, and all of life is holy ground. This remarkable book offers a revival for the soul, a reminder that "we are one with something vast" – a "something" that "is not a thing or a person, but a spiritual source and force at the heart of life."

ISBN 978-1-77343-039-3

5" X 8.5" | 248 PP | PAPERBACK | $19.95

PASSION & PEACE
THE POETRY OF UPLIFT FOR ALL OCCASIONS

COMPILED BY DIANE TUCKER

All cultures we know of, at all times, have had poetry of one sort or another – chants, songs, lullabies, epics, blessings, farewells – to mark life's most important moments, transitions, and transformations. Ever since our species began using words, we have arranged them to please, to experience the pleasures, the fun, of rhythm and rhyme, repetition and pattern. *Passion & Peace: The Poetry of Uplift for All Occasions* was compiled to speak directly to this deep human need, with 120 poems from almost as many classical and contemporary poets, and including a thematic index. A welcome addition to any library and the perfect gift for any occasion, *Passion & Peace* is a heartwarming, uplifting, and inspirational volume.

ISBN 978-1-77343-028-7

6" X 9" | 304 PP | PAPERBACK | $24.95

WOOD LAKE
IMAGINING, LIVING, AND TELLING THE FAITH STORY.

WOOD LAKE IS THE FAITH STORY COMPANY.

It has told
- the story of the seasons of the earth, the people of God, and the place and purpose of faith in the world;
- the story of the faith journey, from birth to death;
- the story of Jesus and the churches that carry his message.

Wood Lake has been telling stories for 40 years. During that time, it has given form and substance to the words, songs, pictures, and ideas of hundreds of storytellers.

Those stories have taken a multitude of forms – parables, poems, drawings, prayers, epiphanies, songs, books, paintings, hymns, curricula – all driven by a common mission of serving those on the faith journey.

WOOD LAKE PUBLISHING INC.
485 Beaver Lake Road
Kelowna, BC, Canada v4v 1s5
250.766.2778

www.woodlake.com